BUT *God...*

This Wasn't My Plan!

CAROL HOPSON

Published by HeartSong Ministries, 1015 Olive Crest Dr.,
Encinitas, CA 92024.

Unless otherwise noted, all scriptures are taken from the New
American Standard Bible, Copyright © 1960, 1963, 1968, 1971,
1972, 1973, 1975, 1977 by the Lockman Foundation. Used by
permission.

ISBN 1-879854-89-9
Library of Congress Catalog Card Number: 99-63457

CONTENTS

CONTENTS

To my husband
Jim

who encouraged me
to write this book...

who has
loved me unconditionally
and selflessly
for 34 years...

who has
lived his life with
integrity, humility
and in obedience to God
in the
midst of all
our
"changed plans"

Chapter 1

THE PLAYHOUSE

There I stood in the middle of the newly built playhouse, thinking of all the many hours of fun my three grandchildren would spend in it. My husband, Jim, had just finished building this adorable structure, complete with window boxes, shutters, electricity, kitchen sink, front deck, carpeted floor, handmade cradle, and more. He had built it on a permanent foundation in our backyard, as we knew we would be there for many years and wanted it to be safe and solid. I was putting some finishing touches in it, such as curtains, dishes, bookshelves, and a table and high chair. My heart was so full of excitement as I thought of my two granddaughters' first sight of their new pretend abode. We had kept it a secret so it would be a total surprise for them.

They usually made the twenty-five-minute drive to our house once or twice a week, and my husband and I were so thankful for the privilege of living near our grandchildren. It was something we had longed for and prayed for as we both felt that our roles as "Nana" and "Papa" were extremely important and special. Our daughter, son-in-law, and one-year-old grandson lived two hours from us and made trips up from their home as often as possible for family gatherings, backyard barbecues, birthdays, and any other reason we could think of. We felt extremely blessed by God!

Jim and I had been married for thirty-one years and had been in Christian school and church ministries for all those years. Fifteen years ago, we had moved to Solvang, California, because God had given us clear direction to start a Christian school in that valley. There was no church to sponsor us, no buildings, no teachers, no students, no money, and no board of directors, but God had told us there was a need there and that we were to step out in faith and He would go before us. So we sold our home, left a large Christian school and a secure position, and with our two junior-high age children, began our walk of faith.

We went door to door in that small town and told people of our plans and asked if they would like to come to an informational meeting to hear about Christian education and what it could mean for their children. At one door, I met a young mother named Sheryl. She had three small daughters, one of which was just about to enter kindergarten. When we told her that we had come to the valley to start a Christian school and asked her if she was interested, she started weeping. "I've been praying for five years that God would raise up a Christian school for my daughters and had almost given up hope," she said. "I can't believe He sent you to my front door."

We had seventy-five people come to our first informational meeting, and one dear man gave us a check for fifteen hundred dollars, which were the first funds we had to begin this venture. Before we had a teacher or student, we bought some books and supplies and salvaged used desks and chalkboards from public and private schools' storage sheds. Without having a facility, we set the date—a date only six weeks away—for our new Christian Academy to open. We needed a minimum of four teachers to begin. We wondered how God would bring them to us, but we were confident He would be faithful.

As we put ads in the local newspaper and continued visiting door to door, we began to get some applications for our "school without a building." We enrolled twenty-two students, who would begin in September, but we had only one teacher and no location yet. Within the next month, God brought three more exceptional teachers to us. So with Jim as the headmaster and me as the secretary and music and drama teacher, we were on our way. Now all we needed was someplace to meet.

Five days before our announced date of opening, a small church vacated its building earlier than its planned moving date. They had built a new facility and were able to advance their move-in date. With hearts of joy and gratitude to our faithful God, we began renovating the rooms in this building on a Saturday morning, with school set to begin on the following Tuesday. With the help of Larry and Nancy Mayfield— dear friends whom God had lead to move to Solvang to help us—and our own two children, we began. We put in partitions, painted walls, cleaned and scrubbed everything, carpeted floors, moved in desks and chairs, put up new lighting, hung chalkboards, decorated bulletin boards, and though we were without sleep, we were ready to begin as scheduled.

What excitement we felt as those first students walked into their classrooms, ready to receive Christ-centered education for the first time. We had no way of knowing how God would provide for salaries, expenses, rent, and more. But, we have an awesome God, and we knew He would expand our faith and stretch us beyond our knowledge if we were faithful and kept our eyes on Him. Within months, the enrollment grew as we endeavored to provide academic excellence combined with reverence for God, respect for our country, honor for and obedience to parents, and biblical character-training. Each year brought more students, more responsibilities, and more challenges, but we were thrilled with what God was doing.

The next years were full of weariness and wonder as we moved ahead—weariness at times as we managed a huge job and overwhelming financial needs, and yet wonder at God's continual provision in the least-expected ways. I remember one day when payroll was due again and we had no money to pay it. Jim and I sat in his office and asked God what He wanted us to do and asked Him to quiet our hearts and help us continue to trust. I returned to my office where a lady was sitting in the chair across from my desk. I didn't recognize her as a parent, so I asked her if I could help her, thinking she might want to enroll a student. She said, "The strangest thing has just happened to me. I've never been in this town before but decided to drive through and see it. There was a detour on the main road, which brought me on this street, and as I saw the sign out front, I knew I had to stop here. As I parked the car, God put it on my heart to write a check for this amount of money and bring it in here. I've never done anything like this before."

As she handed me the check, my eyes were so full of tears that I could hardly make out what she had written. As I blinked through my tears I saw the exact amount that we needed to meet payroll that day! I had never seen a clearer picture of that familiar verse "And my God shall supply all your needs according to His riches in glory in Christ Jesus" (Phil. 4:19). That miracle of God's faithfulness carried us through many more years of difficulty, stretching, and spiritual adventure.

With our exploding enrollment, we needed to find a larger facility. So we began looking around the valley for another building or for land on which we might build. We looked at seventeen different locations over the next few years and were shut down by the planning commission or by problems with permits or high costs. We began to think that we wouldn't be able to expand or grow beyond our present site and decided to rest in what God had already given us. We had so many dedicated families and students and continual excitement about our programs.

The Lord had allowed me to develop and lead the academy's choir, which was the largest children's choir in the valley. We put on Christ-honoring musicals twice a year and invited the whole community to come. As we prepared each musical drama, we prayed for our audience and asked God to use the students' voices, faces, and words to touch hearts and He did. Parents, grandparents, neighbors, and friends found their hearts moved by the children's message in song and by the exuberance with which they shared it. As a result, many people who attended the concerts came to the Lord.

Day by day, month by month, we sought to be faithful to God and not desire more than He had given us in the way of facilities. Then in 1995, after many negotiations and meetings, a major oil company donated an entire school facility to us. It was beyond our greatest dreams. All we had to do was move all the buildings, fences, gymnasium, and playground equipment to a new site. In God's unbelievable ways, He provided us with a beautiful corner lot and the funds to move all of this to our new location in the heart of Solvang. On one day in August, nine trucks made fifty-one trips from the old location to move the buildings through Solvang, to their new home. Some people left for work in the morning with no buildings on that prominent corner and returned home to see an entire school sitting there. You talk about the power of God at work in a community!

As we saw the parking lot being paved, the streetlights going in, the courtyard and walkways being poured, and the plants and shrubs being planted, we were more amazed than ever at God's faithfulness to us. After many years of trying to move the school, God had done the impossible and had given us so much more than we had ever even dreamed. For the first time in fourteen years, we had large, air-conditioned classrooms, spacious offices, workrooms, a gymnasium, and a teacher's lounge. Our computers, which had formerly been in a renovated garage, were now in a state-of-the-art computer lab. The students went from a tiny gravel playground at our former location, to sprawling, green lawns with baseball and soccer fields. Jim and I felt like all of our thirty years of service in various schools, churches, and locations had finally reached a point of incredible fulfillment for us.

Along with this experience, we both had thriving Bible studies we were leading, and we were also involved in a new, exciting, growing church of which we were thrilled to be a part. An older home that needed lots of loving care had caught our eye, and we had totally remodeled it, cleaned up the yard and pool, and added a large barbecue and covered patio for our expanding family. We loved having backyard swims and barbecues for our family and friends and felt this was how it would be for years to come. Especially since we were both in our fifties and thinking that retirement—or at the least, slowing down—was looking more and more inviting. We especially looked forward to being less busy, since the school had now moved to its new location and was well established in the community.

This brings me back to the playhouse. After deciding that we would probably be in this home for many more years, we decided that the playhouse would make a wonderful addition to our backyard enjoyment. However, two weeks after the playhouse was completed, we got a phone call that would change our lives.

CHAPTER 2

THE PHONE CALL

It was a normal Monday morning as I sat in my office at school and answered the phone. A polite gentleman asked to speak to Mr. Hopson. I put my husband on the phone and went about my work. When Jim completed the conversation, he walked into my office and said, "I've just been asked if I would like to apply for the superintendent's position at a large Christian school in the Seattle area."

My heart skipped a beat, and I quickly replied, "Well you told them that you weren't interested, right?"

"Yes," he responded, but I could see he wasn't as adamant about it as

I thought he should be. We talked a little and then put the thought out of our minds until a few weeks later when, again, the school called, asking Jim if he would be willing to fill out a questionnaire and if he would pray about being considered for the position.

We had always desired to do God's will above all else, but this seemed hard even to consider. After all, we had already made a giant leap of faith (in our estimation) when we moved to Solvang and had endured through fifteen years of very hard work to get the school to its present status. We were just now feeling that possibly we could reap the rewards of many years of service. We were also enjoying our grandchildren and our grown children who had moved closer to us and to my parents, who were in their eighties.

Was God asking us to consider leaving everything that was so rewarding to us, everything that was comfortable and everything that brought us so much joy? Why would He do that at this point in our lives? During the times when the school had struggled and financial problems had been overwhelming, we would have been glad to consider a move, but not now—now when our vision had been fulfilled and we could begin really enjoying all God's blessings!

But knowing that the only way to peace is complete obedience, I began praying that I would be open to whatever God asked of me. I began with tears, asking God to forgive me for stubbornly thinking that I deserved to stay where I was just because I was happy, fulfilled, and comfortable. As I began to open my heart to God's heart, I realized that He wouldn't ask this of me without giving me joy in doing it. So my heart began to quiet, and I began my moment-by-moment reliance on Him for peace and direction.

The Phone Call

Waiting

Well, Lord, I'm here again
In this waiting spot.
It seems that learning patience
Is my continual lot.

Isn't there an easier way?
Don't you understand?
All I want is answers now . . .
I want to know your plan.

Waiting, waiting, time lags on.
Why is it so tough?
Why is it that praying hard
Isn't quite enough?

You say you want to teach me,
More patience than before.
You say you want to use me,
To new heights I must soar?

Change my heart, dear Jesus,
And may your will be done.
Change my thoughts, my goals, my dreams,
'Til yours and mine are one.

—Carol Hopson

BUT GOD, THIS WASN'T MY PLAN!

Now, I realize that the thought of moving to a new state doesn't compare with losing a child or a spouse or finding out that you have cancer. But many of us have hopes and dreams, and we've made plans that we hope will work out. We begin getting comfortable and very thankful for where God has allowed us to be. Life is finally going smoothly after many times of struggle and turmoil and we assume that it will continue.

I'm reminded of one of my favorite Old Testament stories found in 2 Chronicles, chapter 20. Jehoshaphat, the King of Judah, was living in peace and prosperity and leading his people to worship God. Things were going well for him and life was good. (I can identify with that.) In a moment, everything changed for him because he received word that the Moabites, Ammonites, and others were coming against him to do battle (vs. 1) All of a sudden, his circumstances had changed, life was uncertain, and he was afraid. I've been afraid many times in my life and can only imagine what was going through Jehoshaphat's mind. He was responsible for all these people—for their safety, their future, their families— and the situation seemed impossible. The armies coming against him were far greater than what he could muster up. But the interesting thing about Jehoshaphat was what he did with his fear. Verse 4 says that "he set himself to seek the Lord." Rather than letting his emotions take over, he sought the Lord—the only one who could help him.

IT HAPPENED AGAIN!

It happened again!
I looked at the circumstances . . .
and I fell.

It happened again!
I listened to some bitter words . . .
and I fell.

It happened again!
I wanted something I couldn't have . . .
and I fell.

It happened again!
I tried to do it by myself . . .
and I fell.

It happened again!
I laid it at my Savior's feet . . .
and I stood.

—Carol Hopson

It seems that Jehoshaphat didn't waste his time and energy on worry, depression, or despair, because he made a choice to turn his heart to the Lord. He also greatly affected those around him by his decision to put the problem on the Lord, and he didn't miss the opportunity God had given him to show God's power in this very difficult circumstance. So rather than have his people all focusing on the impossibility of the situation, they were focusing on the God of the impossible (vs. 3–6)!

Then, rather than let the devil get an entrance through the door of doubt, Jehoshaphat began reminding the people and himself of God's faithfulness and power in the past:

> O Lord God of our father, art not thou God in the heaven and rulest not thou over all the kingdoms of the heathen and in thine hand is there not power and might, so that none is able to withstand thee? Art Thou not our God who didst drive out the inhabitants of this land before thy people Israel, and gavest it to the seed of Abraham thy friend forever? (2 Chron. 20:6–7)

And added to that, Jehoshaphat, as the leader of God's people, affirmed his commitment to God in the middle of the problem. No circumstances had changed: the armies were still coming, his comfort zone had definitely been interrupted, and he didn't have an answer. But again, he made an important choice. After worshiping God in front of the congregation, Jehoshaphat proclaimed, "[We] are powerless before this great multitude who are coming against us; nor do we know what to do, *but our eyes are on Thee*" (vs. 12, emphasis added).

Now, there's something we can all do! It's a choice we can make when faced with interruptions and difficulties. We can choose to keep our eyes on God, and doing that keeps us from focusing on our circumstances. Second Timothy 2:4 states, "No soldier in active service, entangles himself in the affairs of everyday life that he may please the one who enlisted him." Dwelling on the circumstances always entangles us and causes us to stumble in the race, but focusing on the goal (that is, pleasing the Savior) will always bring victory. This victory will be the peace in our hearts because of our right relationship with the Lord. Someone once said, "Nothing can make a trusting Christian fear!" The key word there is *trusting*. If we're trusting, we're not afraid. If we're afraid, we're not trusting.

After God saw what choices Jehoshaphat made, He gave great words of comfort to him through Jahaziel:

> Do not fear or be dismayed because of this great multitude, for the battle is not yours but God's. . . . You need not fight in this battle; station yourselves, stand and see the salvation of the Lord on your behalf, O Judah and Jerusalem. Do not fear or be dismayed; tomorrow go out to face them, for the Lord is with you. (2 Chron. 20:15, 17)

Did you notice that God didn't tell Jehoshaphat what His plan was? He didn't say, "I'm going to defeat them, so don't worry" or "I won't let a single sword touch your people, so don't fear." He simply said, "Do not fear, for the Lord is with you!" That was enough to give peace! Why is that so hard for me? Why do I wonder if I can possibly be happy in a place where I know no one and have no ministries and no family and where it rains a lot but where God will be with me?

Do you wonder how you can be worry-free in your situation? Usually, we think that being worry-free is knowing how everything is going to work out and liking the solution. Then we can trust God! But that isn't trusting; that's having it all figured out and then deciding that what God is going to do is OK with us. What really brings joy to our Father is steadfast obedience in spite of our situation.

"Tomorrow go out and face them" were the next instructions from the Lord. That's not exactly what I feel like doing when I'm worried or afraid or don't like what's going on. It feels better to walk away from the problem rather than deal with it directly. But God says, "Go out and face the problem with Me." Psalm 16:8 is a wonderful passage that tells us how to do just that:

> I have set the Lord continually before me; because He is at my right hand, I will not be shaken.

This means facing our problems *through* the Lord. If I have truly set the Lord continually before me, He is in front of the problem as I view it, and that keeps my focus on Him and His power and ability to deal with my situation. My only responsibility in any area is a right response to His ability.

My favorite part of this story is the ending. I think if I were Jehoshaphat, I would have been forming battle plans, having target practice, and sharpening swords at this point, but Jehoshaphat felt led to assemble a choir, of all things. He instructed them to go out and sing and praise God:

> And when he had consulted with the people, he appointed those who sang to the Lord and those who praised Him in holy attire, as they went out before the army and said, Give thanks to the Lord, for His lovingkindness is everlasting" (v. 21).

Many times I have tried to figure out what God would do or what He should do, and sometimes there just hasn't been any answer that I could see. It seems that Jehoshaphat's situation was like that; he didn't have a battle plan and no other armies were lining up to help him. Humanly speaking, it was an impossible situation. But our God of the impossible showed Himself in an amazing way. For while they were being obedient by praising God,

"...the Lord set ambushes against the sons of Ammon, Moab, and Mount Seir, who had come against Judah; so they were routed. For the sons of Ammon and Moab rose up against the inhabitants of Mount Seir destroying them completely, and when they had finished with the inhabitants of Seir, they helped to destroy one another. When Judah came to the lookout of the wilderness, they looked toward the multitude; and behold, they were corpses lying on the ground, and no one had escaped." (see vs. 22–24)

You know, in all of my imaginations, I never would have dreamed up that ending! That's what is so exciting about keeping our eyes on God and watching what He's going to do. The enemies actually turned on each other and killed each other without Jehoshaphat's people lifting a weapon. They were involved only in worship and praise and left the impossible to God. Can you imagine how their faith in God increased and what stories spread throughout the land (see v. 29)? There were also great blessings because of their obedience. First, they were able to take all the spoils from the fallen armies, which took them three days to collect. And secondly, their kingdom was rewarded with peace (vs. 25–30).

As I pondered this story, I knew that God could do the impossible for me, too, but I had to be willing to worship and praise in the midst of this decision-making process or I would miss an opportunity to be used by Him and possibly miss His leading.

BUT GOD, THIS WASN'T MY PLAN!

GOD OF THE IMPOSSIBLE

My God of the impossible, a wondrous truth that is!
For problems that I can't work out, aren't mine to solve, but His!

I cannot comprehend the love that He bestows on me.
He's taken all my sin and guilt and left me feeling free.

At moments I forget this truth and carry my burden bag.
Then how hopeless things can seem, and life becomes a drag.

There is no joy in little things, no peace within my heart.
And life seems just unbearable each day, right from the start.

Why do I choose to live this way, when God is always there,
to lift my load and strengthen me and claim me as His heir?

I choose because I've gone adrift and left my anchor strong.
I've taken things in my own hands and everything goes wrong!

I'll set my mind on things above and what God's pow'r can do.
The battle is not mine to win for He will see me through.

So thank you God for your great love, your power and your
might.
Forgive me for my selfish ways; I now give up my fight.

My God of the impossible, a wondrous truth that is!
For problems that I can't work out aren't mine to solve, but His!

—Carol Hopson

My heart was telling me that we were already serving the
Lord right where we were and there was no reason to even
consider this move. But I had prayed to God—because of

how comfortable and happy I was—that He would make it so clear to us if ever He wanted us to leave our ministry in Solvang. I asked that He would bring someone knocking on our front door so I'd know it was from Him. I had asked almost jokingly, but also seriously because of my desire to know God's will.

CHAPTER 3

MY ATTITUDE

J im received the questionnaire from Seattle, took a couple of weeks to fill it out, and told them we were not looking to move but would remain open to the Lord's leading. When we received a phone call asking if someone could come visit us in Solvang, we said yes, as long as they understood that we still were not making any commitment to them. We were excited to show whomever came down, what miracles God had brought about in our school.

But weeks later, when three people from Seattle—people whom we'd never met—came walking up our front walkway and knocked on our door, I realized God might just be answering my very definite prayer for direction, and I was overwhelmed. After several hours with these wonderful people, we knew we could no longer push this to the back of our minds. We needed to face it with the Lord and without fear, as Jehoshaphat did. We agreed to fly to Seattle to see the work there and allow the Lord to lead both them and us.

It was at this time that the Lord did some incredible work in my heart through His precious Word. I began studying the second chapter of Philippians where Paul wrote,

> Have this attitude in yourselves which was also in Christ Jesus, who, although He existed in the form of God, did not regard equality with God a thing to be grasped, but emptied Himself, taking the form of a bondservant, and being made in the likeness of men. And being found in appearance as a man, He humbled Himself by becoming obedient unto the point of death, even death on a cross. (Phil. 2:5-8)

There were three things that jumped out at me right away. They weren't new to me, and they're probably not new to you, but the Lord was using His living Word to reach my heart and make it line up with His.

GIVING UP MY RIGHTS

The first attitude Jesus had was one of not grasping His rights. He had a right to be God—to be honored, not humiliated; to be revered, not resented. But He chose, in His humility and obedience, to give up His rights to everything. What an example for me! In my most human and selfish moments, I was thinking that I had a right to stay where I was and enjoy life in my secure surroundings where I received lots of positive feedback and had lots of friends. I had a right to be where people knew me and asked me to speak frequently at conventions, retreats, and seminars; a right to keep leading my 150-voice children's choir, which I had begun fifteen years earlier with only twelve small voices. I had a right to be near my children and grandchildren because I could have an impact on their lives. And I had a right not to step out in faith again because I had already done that.

I remember another time when I argued my rights before God. It was three months after we had begun our new "faith school" and Jim had been stricken with severe back problems. At this point, in a brand new school, we were doing everything. While I was printer, bookkeeper, secretary, nurse, counselor, choir director, Bible-study leader, and drama coach, Jim was principal, fundraiser, board trainer, janitor, maintenance worker, playground builder, chapel speaker, and anything else that came up. To say we had to be flexible and versatile was an understatement.

Now, to have Jim flat in bed and unable to walk, and the school just into its third month seemed more than I could deal with. I figured God would heal him quickly and this ordeal would soon be over and I could give Him the glory for seeing us through yet another difficult circumstance. But God had different plans, and Jim was down for six weeks before we finally found a doctor that knew what he needed. Then we were facing back surgery and uncertainty about the outcome. The doctor warned me that Jim could be paralyzed if a slight slip occurred, that he could have bone cancer or a different debilitating disease, or that it might be a disc problem that they could possibly fix. How could God put me through this when we had just stepped out in faith to start this work?

Jim had the surgery and it was a disc problem that was effectively treated. He would be able to return home in five more days, and I couldn't wait. I desperately wanted my best friend back and wanted him to be my strength again. But just when I thought the worst was almost over (as I was trying to run everything at school, drive forty miles each way to the hospital every day to spend time with my husband, and return home to kids, homework, phone calls, and school problems), I received a call from the hospital. Jim was one day away from coming home, and he had gotten a staph infection in the wound, and doctors couldn't find the right antibiotic for it. I was told that he was on a twenty-four-hour alert, as his fever was extremely high, and that they had to find the correct medication within the next twenty-four hours or he might not make it.

There I lay, at one o'clock in the morning, in my fear and misery, pleading with God about my rights. "Is this fair?" I asked. "I only want to serve You, Lord, and now this? Don't I have a right to a healthy husband after all I've endured these past weeks and months? How can I run this school by myself? Do You really see my situation, Lord?" Then I began meditating on what my purpose in life was. It was to glorify God in whatever situation He chose for me. It was easy to do that when things were going well, but it was so much more difficult when it might mean losing my husband.

ANYTHING YOU SAY, LORD!

Anything you say, Lord,
I heard a preacher say.
How wonderful and servantlike
For him to live that way!

I think I'll try it, Lord;
It sounds so free of care
To let things happen as You plan
And see how I will fare.

Oh, wait a minute, Lord,
You can't take that away!
For it's one thing I really need
To get me through each day.

Did You somehow forget
That I'm not strong like You?
I can't take all this pressure
And to You still be true.

Oh, Lord, I can't believe it,
You cannot ask me this.
Could it be Your plans for me
Have somehow gone amiss?

Anything You say, Lord,
I heard a preacher say.
But now I know that only God
Can help me live that way.

—Carol Hopson

I prayed in earnest that night that God would somehow let me know that He would see me through this dark place. I needed something tangible to hang on to as I felt that I was at the end of my endurance. As I was wiping my tears, my bedroom door opened and my eleven-year-old daughter, Jennifer, walked in. She never got up in the night, so I it really surprised me to see her. She said, "Mom, are you awake? I need to tell you something. I was reading the Bible just before I went to bed and I wanted to share this verse with you, but I fell asleep. It's 'My grace is sufficient for you.' That's the part I remember. Goodnight mom and I love you."

It was like God had picked me up in his loving arms, right there in my bedroom and had whispered those very words in my ears, and I was immediately at rest. The worry and fear were gone and God's wondrous grace took over. They did find the right medication for Jim's infection the next day, and in three weeks he was back to work with a recycled back that has kept him upright and fairly healthy for the last seventeen years.

But, here I was again, grasping my rights, as if I'd earned them. And God in His patient and loving way kept working on my heart, and I began to put those rights at Jesus feet and leave the future with Him.

CHAPTER 4

THE OPPORTUNITY

As we flew in to Sea-Tac airport, I was amazed at how green and lush everything was. (I was told there was a reason for that!) There was water everywhere, and it was so much more beautiful than I had expected. As we met with the faculty and board, we were moved by their dedication and warmth and felt a definite tug on our hearts. But it was still difficult to consider such a big move, because nothing was familiar and we'd have to start all over in every area of our lives. When you're in your fifties, that's not always an exciting thing to face. We also didn't understand why God needed us there. Why didn't they call someone else who was looking to move or specifically wanted that job?

Emptying Self

As we sat on the plane and headed home, it became clear to me that the next attitude I had discovered in Philippians, chapter 2, was needed in my life. Paul said that Jesus had "emptied Himself." I began pondering what He had emptied Himself of—His desires, the power of His deity, and what He would like to have avoided. Remember His prayer in Matthew 26:39 when He prayed, "My Father, if it is possible, let this cup pass from Me; yet not as I will, but as Thou wilt"? He was emptying self and replacing it with His Father's will, and that prepared Him for the task ahead.

Carole Carlson, in her book *Corrie ten Boom, Her Life, Her Faith*, wrote the following story:

> One time Betsy was vulnerable to the misery surrounding her; the conditions were designed to break the strongest spirits. At 3:30 A.M. they were driven from their beds, to stand for roll call in the Lagerstrasse. Ravensbruck at that time contained 35,000 people, a sickening sea of wraithlike humanity. Finally, numb with cold in the German winter, the siren sounded to fall out. But the barracks door was locked, and for another forty-five minutes they were kept in the cold, with the *aufseherin* guarding the door with a whip. A woman tried to crawl through a window and was beaten unmercifully, while the others watched, petrified with misery.
>
> Betsy leaned against her beloved sister and whispered, "Oh, Corrie, this is hell." Courage is born in adversity, but Corrie said she was not brave, that she often pulled her dirty blanket over herself and prayed, "Lord, I am weak

and cowardly and of little faith; hold me close. Thou art the conqueror. Give me courage." From that dependence, that surrender to her Lord, Corrie accomplished feats that were astounding for a woman in her fifties, weakened by malnutrition and ill-treatment.

One night she heard that 250 younger, stronger Dutch prisoners were being transported to a distant factory; destination unknown, return uncertain. In the middle of the night, Corrie went to the washroom, climbed out the window, and stationed herself in the pitch dark in a place where she was sure the prisoners would pass. She prayed, "Lord give me some word for them." As each one passed she whispered,

"Jesus is Victor."

"Oh Corrie, how could you? Go back to your barracks."

"Fear not; only believe."

"Thank you, Corrie, God bless you."

"Underneath us are the everlasting arms."

Corrie told Betsy later, "The Holy Spirit gave me a short message for everyone who went through the gate." She risked being cruelly punished or killed but was rewarded after the war when she found out that of the 250, only one did not come back to Holland. A survivor told her later; "Shortly after we arrived, a terrible bombardment shook the area. I was sitting in a corner of a room and couldn't think of anything except what you said; "Jesus is Victor." We were unprotected, but our building was not bombed."

Courage does not depend on circumstances, but on the relationship that remains during the circumstances."

Corrie had learned the secret of emptying self so that she could be used by God. I'm sure there were many plans she had made that didn't fit this picture. Even in these horrible surroundings she could have thought of self and, staying in her bed, of not going out in the cold, of not getting caught and punished. But the higher calling was to lay down self's desires and take up the Lord's desires.

As we flew over the houses, lakes, trees, and cities, I remembered a song that the Bill Gaither Vocal Band used to sing about needing a new point of view. I knew I wanted that new point of view, but to get it, I had to do some emptying. These are the things God pointed out to me as I prayerfully asked for His wisdom:

- I needed to give up my plans and dreams of what I thought would make me happy.
- I needed to be content with His plan for me.
- I needed to be steadfast in my faith.
- I needed to be an example to others in the midst of the process, not wait until the process was over.
- I needed to make obedience to Him, rather than my right to be near my grandchildren, my top priority.
- I needed to trust in His love for me, period!

As the Holy Spirit worked on me in these areas, my prayer had to be "Lord, I give up all the things that seem so important to me and all the ministries You've given me here, and I walk on in faith that You have a plan for me because You love me."

As you consider your situation, could it be that you might have a need to empty self? What has a tight hold on your heart? What might God ask of you to which you would say, "I can't"? What is entangling you in your everyday life right now? Is it financial stability, closeness of family, a secure future, friendships? Maybe it's your dreams that haven't worked out and you're holding a grudge or growing a seed of bitterness because of it. If this is the case, you won't be open to the Holy Spirit's leading, and you might miss a tremendous opportunity that God has for you.

Paul reminded the Colossian believers,

> [W]e have not ceased to pray for you and to ask that you may be filled with the knowledge of His will in all spiritual wisdom and understanding, so that you may walk in a manner worthy of the Lord, to please Him in all respects, bearing fruit in every good work and increasing in the knowledge of God. (1:9–10)

The goal is to "walk in a manner *worthy* of the Lord and to *please Him* in all respects" (emphasis added). Sometimes we get so caught up in pleasing ourselves or others, in the midst of our chosen service, and forget what our goal really is. And sometimes God has to use powerful means to get our attention.

CHAPTER 5

THE
DECISION

God had our full attention by now. When Jim received the call telling him that the board felt he was the right person for the position in Seattle, we stepped into the third attitude of Philippians 2, the attitude of humble obedience!

HUMBLE OBEDIENCE

"Jesus humbled himself by becoming obedient to the point of death, even death on a cross" (see v. 8). All God was asking of me was to be obedient unto moving! That seems so small in comparison, and yet in my world, it seemed huge. God had definitely been working on Jim and on me to prepare us for this moment, and when it came we knew, without a doubt, that God was calling us to Seattle. That doesn't mean that it became easy or painless, but with the decision to say yes to God, came His amazing peace.

PEACE

Peace, what is it?
Some ethereal feeling . . .
Is it freedom from cares and hurts and scars?
Is it wounds that don't need healing?

Peace, what is it?
A jovial, trivial smile . . .
Is it never needing to shed a tear?
Is it happiness all the while?

Peace, what is it?
A strength we can't understand.
It's living and feeling and knowing
that God has ahold of your hand!

—Carol Hopson

I felt a little like my son Jeff, when he was four years old and was climbing up a trail at Yosemite. The trail was steep and narrow and quite dangerous, but when we reached the top, I asked Jeff if he was scared. He quickly replied, "'Course not, Mommy, Daddy was holding my hand!" What a simple picture of peace and security. It was so incredible to me to allow God to work in my heart to bring me to this point of peace. I learned that the first two attitudes in Philippians chapter two were truly essential if peace was to be the end product. If the Holy Spirit hadn't convicted me of giving up my rights for my love of the Lord, and then emptying the things that had a hold on my heart, I couldn't have been open to His leading and couldn't have walked through the next two months in His peace.

Many times during the next few weeks, the move didn't make sense to us or to others we knew and loved. Why would God have us leave a vital, growing, exciting ministry for unknown territory? But because of the steps we'd taken together and because of God's specific leading and the peace we felt, we never wavered from our decision. Our children and parents were extremely supportive and also felt that it was God's will for us, even though it brought sadness to each one. My parents, in their eighties, felt sure this was what God wanted and encouraged us to go, rather than think of their own needs and desires. It was so helpful to see God work in their hearts to free us to go and even encourage us to accept God's plan.

As I look back over our years of ministry, I recall another time when this peace was especially present in difficult circumstances. Jim was teaching in a Christian school and we had two small children, a house payment, a car payment, and other bills each month. The school was going through financial difficulties and couldn't pay their teachers for several months. Some urged us to leave the work, but Jim and I felt called to this ministry. And so Jim mowed lawns and cleaned buildings after teaching all day, and I gave piano lessons and had regular garage sales. During this time, we prayed for God's peace and direction so that we would be a witness of His grace. It would be so easy to let worry take over, but we knew that wasn't what God wanted of us.

One afternoon, I told Jim that we had very little food left and no money and no savings. We decided to go to the Lord alone with our concern. We had been expecting a check any day and thought things would be all right anytime soon. But time dragged on, and things looked bleak. We prayed and asked the Lord to provide for our needs in His way and asked for His peace. Then we locked up the house and walked to the park with our children. We had decided to leave our needs with the Lord and just go enjoy being together. When we returned, an hour later, we unlocked the door and went inside. As I entered the kitchen, my eyes fell on the kitchen table. There I saw a one hundred dollar bill, just lying there. I yelled for Jim and the kids to come and see it, as I had never had one in my possession before. To this day, the only explanation is that God put it there! What a miracle God gave us and our teachable children. God gave us His peace and provided for our needs. From that point on, it became easier to trust Him for our daily provision.

MIRACLES

Do you look for miracles in everyday affairs?
They're there!

Do you think some things are luck
that brighten up your day?
When problems fade and people change
and children grow
and flowers bloom
and night comes on
and trees stand tall
and you are loved . . .
forgiv'n of all.

Do you look for miracles in everyday affairs?
They're there!

—Carol Hopson

The peace that "surpasses all comprehension" was a gift from God that He promises to each of us when we take our worries to Him:

Be anxious [worried] for nothing, but in everything by prayer and supplication with thanksgiving, let your requests be made known to God. And the peace which surpasses all comprehension, shall guard your hearts and your minds in Christ Jesus. (Phil. 4:6–7)

CHAPTER 6

THE SHIELD OF FAITH

Oh how my heart needed guarding! You might ask what it needed guarding from? I'm quick to tell you that it needed guarding from Satan's attacks at my weakest points. Whenever I'd think of leaving my home and my friends, my heart needed guarding. When I'd see my grandchildren playing in the playhouse and knew that it would end very soon, I could feel Satan on the warpath. And when I thought of leaving the sunshine and all that was comfortable and familiar for the unknown, I could easily get discouraged. Even after the peace God gave and the clear direction from the Lord, I was still vulnerable if I let my shield down. We are warned in Ephesians 6:16 to "take up the shield of faith with which you will be able to extinguish all the flaming missiles of the evil one." I had taught this many times to others and felt I had a good grip on it, but I definitely had to be taking up the shield on a moment-by-moment basis if I was to remain steadfast. I noticed three things about this verse that really helped me.

TAKING UP THE SHIELD

First of all, it was *my* responsibility to take up the shield. I needed to be actively involved in prayer and reading God's Word in order to keep my shield in place. This is one reason I strongly believe in scripture memorization. Satan seems to attack me when I'm not near my Bible and not praying, so I need to have the shield of God's Word in my heart to call on immediately. I needed to recall God's words in Proverbs 3:5: "Trust in the Lord with all your heart and lean not on your own understanding." God's plan didn't make sense to me and I didn't understand why He wanted to move us, but that's why I needed to claim this verse over and over. I wasn't to trust in *my understanding* but in *God's leading*. Even well-meaning friends will try to point out that a certain situation doesn't seem sensible. We certainly heard that when we moved to Solvang to start a school without a sponsoring church, a board, a building, or teachers. But God's ways often don't make sense to the human heart, and I believe that's why it brings such joy to the Lord when we obey in spite of not understanding why or how.

Another verse I learned in my childhood was "Thy Word have I treasured in my heart that I may not sin against Thee" (Ps. 119:11). Now, I had seen children memorize a good number of scriptures so they could get grades or awards, but often these same children chose to sin when the opportunity was there. So what does this verse mean? We need to know what the word *treasured* refers to in this verse. A more accurate version would read, "God's word have I read, studied, meditated on, and decided to obey, that I might not sin against God." There's the difference! The child who memorizes but doesn't practice it, has it only in his head. *The believer who memorizes, meditates on and decides to obey, has it in his heart.* That believer is ready to put up the shield of faith from his or her knowledge and application of God's Word, and Satan is defeated.

If our shield of faith is in place we won't be experiencing the "deadly Ds" of discontent, distrust of God's plan, doubting God's provision, disobedience, despair, or discouragement. It's important to note, however, that the shield doesn't keep Satan from attacking, but it will keep his attacks from wounding or defeating us.

Secondly, I noted that the "flaming missiles of the evil one" were darts, or missiles, of swift and undiscerned flight, intended to inflict deep wounds on the soul. The "undiscerned flight" stood out to me because I realized Satan would attack when and where I least expected it or when I was least prepared. This warning and promise is often overlooked or not taken seriously, and the evil one has an open target. As I've reflected on those fiery darts, I've discovered some of Satan's tricks in my own life over the years.

THE DECEIVING DART

The *deceiving dart* is one of his favorite weapons. Revelation 12:9 reminds us that he "deceives the whole world." "I'm not pretty"; "I'm not useful"; "I'm not talented"; and "I'm not appreciated" are all in his weaponry. If he can get us to have a low self-image, then he can minimize or even squelch our enthusiasm to serve the Lord. He'll deceive us into thinking we're not good enough, and there'll be someone else who can do it. Being a church pianist for many years, I had the opportunity (or challenge) of playing many offertories, and it seemed that Satan really enjoyed working on me during the prayer right before I was to play. I'd have thoughts, such as "I'm not ready"; "No one will appreciate all the hard work I've done if I make a mistake"; "So-and-so could play it better"; and so on. I had to practice putting my shield up before each offertory and just give each one to the Lord as my worship of Him. Then the devil had no way to hurt me.

Another way Satan defeats us is by getting us to think that we don't have to obey all of God's Word, we may have the idea that other Christians don't, and they're doing OK. "I'm just not comfortable sharing my faith" is a common disclaimer among believers. Or "I know I'm not supposed to yell at my kids, but anger is just my thing" or "It's how we handle things in our family." Somehow with these arguments, all the scriptures dealing with anger get thrown out the window for convenience's sake (see Eph. 4:29 and Col. 3:8–17). Or our mind starts thinking that we'd be happy if only we had a different mate or different children, a different job or more money. This subtle trap of wrong thinking grows and grows until we don't realize how many excuses we're making for not having the joy God intended us to have and for not sharing it with others. Someone has said, "Contentment comes, not from great wealth, but from few wants." *Understanding that lasting joy comes, not from right circumstances, but from a right relationship with the Lord, puts the shield in place and extinguishes the darts of deceit.*

Paul warned believers in Colossians 2:8:

> See to it that no one takes you captive through philosophy and empty deception, according to the tradition of men, according to the elementary principles of the world, rather than according to Christ.

Satan would love to take Christians minds captive in the area of raising children. If he can get Christian parents to disregard biblical discipline for their children and go with the "tradition of men" and the empty ideas of the world, he has scored a real victory. Parents are being deceived all the time by listening to so-called experts on raising children—"experts" who don't have any regard for what the Creator of the child says. We must continually be on guard about what the media and the world around us are saying, and we must know what God's Word teaches. Then we must be diligent to believe it and practice it.

THE DOUBTING DART

The second dart Satan has used in my life is the *doubting dart*. Remember how he got Eve to doubt what God had told her and caused her to doubt God's righteousness?

> And the serpent said to the woman, "You shall not surely die, for God knows that in the day you eat from it your eyes will be opened and you will be like God, knowing good and evil." (Gen 3:4)

He twisted God's motives, thereby causing doubt in Eve. Sometimes we can doubt the truth of God's Word because we don't see it working. We're tempted to think that our prayers aren't being heard because we're not getting the answer we've been waiting for. Or we doubt that we need to forgive someone again and again because we get tired of forgiving, and the person doesn't seem to change. At times I've doubted whether or not I wanted to continue speaking and giving seminars, because Satan certainly has his ways of attacking through criticism and discouragement.

DOES IT REALLY MATTER?

Does it really matter what I do and what I say?
Do I always have to guard my words and actions every day?

I just don't think I want to be a leader, not right now.
'Cause then I can't complain and question you on why and
how.
I'd like at least a day or two to feel a little bitter.
Or maybe I could try out what it's like to be a quitter.

I wonder what it feels like to just sit and sulk awhile?
And let those unkind thoughts continue, mile after mile.

But I can't seem to find a verse to let me go this route.
So, I guess I'll need to trust You, Lord, to work this whole
thing out!

—Carol Hopson

Be steadfast, immovable, always abounding in the work
of the Lord, for as much as you know that your labor is
not in vain in the Lord. (1 Cor. 15:58)

God doesn't say to be steadfast only when things go right,
and He doesn't say to be immovable only if we don't have

doubts. It's a direct command and warning to remain true to what we know about God and His faithfulness.

Sometimes we doubt God because circumstances pile up when we're trying to keep our focus right, and we just feel unable to deal with them. While we were going through the difficulties and emotions of preparing for the move, I acquired a severe pain in my shoulder, which caused me some concern. It became more and more painful to just move my arm or sleep, and I realized that it wasn't going away, so I went to the doctor. It took a month of seeing three different doctors before I was told that I needed an MRI because they suspected something very abnormal. *Here we go again*, I thought. *Isn't it enough that I'm dealing with the move and explaining it to all our friends and selling the house (and playhouse) and ending our ministries and seeing our grandchildren for the last time?*

Of course, I thought of cancer! What does God want from me now? Would He lead us to this whole new ministry and take us through all these emotions only to find out that I'm dying? (You can tell that the doubts were there as I began jumping to lots of conclusions.) How thankful I am that God graciously brought my thinking back to a reliance on Him and a willingness for whatever He asked of me. As I faced the MRI, I asked God to use it in some specific way if He chose, and I would be a willing vessel.

THE DAY OF THE MRI

Well, Lord, I'm going in today
to have an MRI.
It's not just what I wanted,
but on You I will rely.

BUT GOD, THIS WASN'T MY PLAN!

I've heard some awful things
about just being in that tube
And if I didn't know your peace
I don't know what I'd do.

The time has come to lay right down
and put You to the test.
I'm doing what the doctor said,
now Lord, please do the rest.

It's not so bad inside of here;
it's clean and fresh and light,
And not so very scary, but . . .
it is a little tight!

Now, Lord, I'm going to sing some songs,
not loud, but in my heart.
And keep my mind on praising You
each moment from the start.

It sounds like I'm inside a pipe
with someone banging loud,
But I prefer to think
I'm really resting on a cloud.

Oh no, dear Lord, I have to cough,
I'm not supposed to move.
So I am going to ask You Lord,
the urge to cough remove.

I knew that you could do it, Lord;
the urge has gone away.
I didn't have to call for help,

THE SHIELD OF FAITH

just trust You and obey.

I wonder how long it has been
since this ordeal began?
I've sung a lot and thought and prayed
and even a poem planned.

How timely that our Bible study
this week deals with stress,
And God is causing me to grow
by going through this test.

It just can't be, what words of bliss,
coming through these holes:
"It's over, Mrs. Hopson.
You may get up and go!"

Out I slide, as smooth as glass,
on a conveyer belt.
The room seems large and spacious
and I've never better felt.

What did I learn from all of this,
what lesson was in store?
That trusting God to calm my heart
brought peace and so much more.

I learned we have two choices,
when faced with fear or stress.
We either choose to deny God's power
or in Him truly rest!

—Carol Hopson

After ten more days of waiting and more x rays, they determined that I had a frozen shoulder and needed extensive physical therapy or it would get worse. God's timing is always so interesting to me, but I've learned not to try to figure it out. I just needed to fit this into my schedule and deal with it and see how God would use it. At least I wasn't dying!

It amazed me how many people I ran into who were going to have an MRI shortly. Each one expressed worry or fear in some way and needed encouragement or someone to pray for them. I also learned that many people were watching me to see if God could give me peace in this situation too. In the past months I've been privileged to share this particular experience—and especially the poem—with doctors, nurses, patients, and friends, and God has answered my prayer of using even this to glorify Him. If Satan would have been free to keep me doubting God's power and purpose in this situation, I would have experienced defeat and discouragement, rather than experiencing God's great love for me..

THE UNDOING DART

The third dart that Satan uses is the *undoing dart.* In the Book of Mark, we read,

When the word is sown and they hear, immediately Satan comes and takes away the word which has been sown in them. . . . And others are the ones on whom the seed was sown among thorns; these are the ones who have heard the word and the worries of the world and deceitfulness of riches, and the desires for other things enter in and choke the word, and it becomes unfruitful. (4:15, 18–19)

Satan loves to sneak in and undo what God wants to do or has done through a sermon, a devotional, a retreat, or some other message from His Word. It's amazing how one phone call, one comment, one circumstance can change our focus and rob us of our joy, and then Satan has accomplished his purpose of undoing! Colossians 3:2 says, "Set your mind on things above, not on things of the earth." We are told to set our mind on spiritual things, not on earthly circumstances. But how do we do that? We obey by asking, "What does God want me to do in this situation? How can I be obedient in spite of what's happened? Do I really want to give Satan a victory in my life?" Then I can ask God to help me focus on what I *can* do, not on what I *can't* do. Remember Jehoshaphat? He knew he couldn't defeat three armies, but he chose to focus on what he could do—obey God by trusting and praising Him in the midst of the problem and leave the battle to Him (see 2 Chron. 20).

After studying about Satan's darts, or missiles, I recalled that the verse says that the shield will "extinguish *all* the flaming missiles of the evil one" (emphasis added). There is nothing that can reach us unless we let the shield down. There is nothing that can penetrate the shield. If something or someone has reached me and has caused discouragement or doubt, it is because I haven't kept the shield of faith in place, and Satan has taken the opportunity to strike a blow.

Have You Misplaced Your Shield of Faith?

Have you misplaced your shield today?
Did Satan strike a blow?
Did worry, fear, or doubt set in?
Just where did your faith go?

You've heard God's Words; they're very clear:
"Stand firm, be on your guard!"
But having faith when under fire
Is sometimes very hard.

Again God's loving, gentle voice says,
"Child take up your shield."
And once again you realize
That you forgot to yield.

So let's start out in obedience
As each new day we face,
And watch God give us victory
As we keep our shield in place!

—Carol Hopson

Again, obedience is the key to keeping the shield in place.
Obedience in believing that God is in control, that God is
faithful, and that He will see me through this time, just as
He has done in the past. Isn't obedience what we're always

trying to teach our children, and we use many different ways and experiences to teach it to them? That's just how our heavenly Father lovingly teaches us, through the choices that we make. When we choose to rely on our emotions, our shield comes down, and we are vulnerable again.

CHAPTER 7

THE MOVE

God had taken me through many stages and His Word had spoken to me and answered my needs time and time again. As Jim and I followed the call of the Lord on our hearts day by day, we accepted the call to Seattle and began the process of uprooting, both physically and emotionally. How we praised the Lord that our children and their spouses and our parents were in total agreement that this was the Lord's plan for us and that we needed to obey no matter how difficult it would be for everyone.

Through the farewells and the packing, God granted us such grace and kept us focused on "forgetting what lies behind and reaching forward to what lies ahead" (Phil. 3:13). I really didn't know what was ahead, but I knew His peace! As we arrived in Seattle, we still had no idea why God had moved us there, but Jim began his job as superintendent of a large Christian school system and was extremely busy getting acquainted with the staff, parents, students, and the entire system. Meanwhile, I was unpacking and trying to make our new residence look like home.

I had never been in a situation where I knew no one and didn't know the area and had no position in a church or school and no family at home. As I emptied box after box of belongings, I wondered, *Who am I now?* In Solvang I was the secretary and cofounder of the Christian Academy. I was Nana to my grandchildren and Mom to my kids and their spouses. I was choir director and Bible-study leader, counselor and friend, but who was I now? As loneliness entered my experience for the first time that I could ever remember, I began to see my life as a book in which the pages, up to this point, had been so very full. I had filled each one to the brim with good things—with helping others and working and spending time with my grandchildren—but they were indeed full! As I visualized them, there was no room on my pages for God to add anything. And as I sat in my new surroundings, I saw a new chapter with blank pages. As I asked God for wisdom, He spoke to my heart: "*Carol, you are my servant, my child, and that is enough! Let me fill your blank pages with what I have in store for you.*"

"Not that I speak from want; for I have learned to be content in whatever circumstances I am" (Phil. 4:11). Contentment began to fill my heart as I continued my daily routines, and I was eager to see what God was going to write on my pages each day. I spent long hours in studying His Word for my own growth and in preparing seminars from my experiences, though I was without a place to share them. For years I had been asked to speak at Christian-school conventions and church retreats and women's conferences. But no one knew me in Washington, and so that, too, had been left behind in my book of full pages.

I prayed each morning that God would use me as He saw fit, wherever I was and with whomever He chose. I had no idea how that would happen, but I was willing to find out. One day, I ventured out to the local mall, with map in hand, and stopped in a small coffee shop for a latté (a Seattle custom I had learned). As I ordered my drink, I noticed the despair in the employee's voice and asked her if she was all right. "No," she replied and went on to say that "life sucks!" I knew that this was God's handwriting on my page as I began talking to her about her problem and about how there was a God who loved her and wanted to help her through all her problems. She was so open and receptive, and at the end, she promised to go to church and learn more. It was about a twenty-minute conversation, but I could tell that she had renewed hope, and I was so thankful to see how God could use me even in a coffee shop.

I began to see His writing more clearly each day, sometimes in talking with a neighbor or encouraging someone in the grocery store. During the first few weeks after the move, I became keenly aware of the needs of the strangers around me, and there were numerous opportunities to share God's love or offer an invitation to church or just smile and encourage someone. But since we had moved in October, the winter months had set in. It was totally different from what I was used to in California, and again, I had to make daily choices as to whether to complain about it or accept it with joy.

CHOICES

I have a choice to make today.
The sky is, oh, so dark,
And I'm so used to sunny days
And walking in the park.

In sunshine there's so much to do
But what to do in rain?
I don't think that the Lord has planned
For me to just complain.

What blessings can I claim right now
When outside grows so dim?
Is happiness a product of sun
Or a relationship with Him?

I know God gives me choices
That will change my attitude.
I know I need to look to Him
To show me what to do.

I think I'll choose obedience
And get my will in line.
There's reading, writing, and calls to make
And making the most of my time.

I called a friend whose faith grew dim
And reminded her to trust,
And realized that on gloomy days
Helping others is a must!

I wrote some notes of encouragement
To those I felt in need,

And read a chapter in The Book
My hungry soul to feed.

And then I took a walk to see
A neighbor on my street.
How could I be God's servant if
My neighbors I don't meet?

Her lonely heart was yearning
For someone who really cared.
But had it been a sunny day
I might have not been there.

There's something God is teaching me
About these days of rain,
To let Him fill my days with joy
And from discontent refrain.

—Carol Hopson

After about two months of learning to be content with just being God's servant, the Lord began to open doors that I would never have expected. I was asked to do Christmas seminars in churches and in Christian schools on the topic of "Preparing your Heart and Home for a Christ-Centered Christmas." I was so excited for the opportunity to share and have a ministry of my own that God, not I, had planned. The months that followed, opened numerous doors for speaking at church luncheons and retreats and for beginning a mother's Bible study. It seemed miraculous to me because I didn't know how these people knew that I had a passion for sharing the Word with women. I could only figure that God had told them, and He was showing me how He would use

His servant when the time was right and when I'd learned contentment in the change of plans for my life.

As my pages filled with speaking and teaching, God began to write in times for meeting with school moms who needed counseling or encouragement, neighbors who needed a friend, and families who needed God's direction for their problems. My days were also filled with school events and with supporting my husband in many areas of the ministry. Another page was filled with plans to take twenty-four high-school students to Korea on a mission trip. I couldn't ever have imagined the joy of working with these young, moldable, impressionable lives. Each day had so many opportunities to share, one-on-one or collectively, about the things God had been teaching me and was continuing to teach me.

We had been on tour in Korea for six days and had a very rich, widespread ministry with churches, hospitals, colleges, high schools, and schools for the disabled. Jim preached several places, and the students shared their testimonies over and over, and the light and love of Jesus was on their faces as they sang each concert and shared each word. One night, after a very difficult, full schedule of singing and witnessing, the students were scheduled to go to Korean homes to sleep and experience the culture firsthand. However, they had been in Seoul for six days and were exhausted and not used to the food and sleeping conditions, and I heard grumbling about not wanting to go to the homes because of fatigue and discomfort.

As I asked God for wisdom, He prodded me to share my testimony about moving to Seattle and leaving my comfort zone and all the things that I thought brought me joy and about how Jim and I had decided to step out in obedience even though we didn't feel like it. I went on to share the joy of obedience that God had brought into my life and gave specific examples, one of which was being on this trip with them. I asked them to put God to the test and go to the homes with an open heart and ask God to show them the joy of obedience. As they went to meet their eager hosts, my husband and I prayed that God would show them a lesson that they could carry with them through life.

The next morning, we anxiously awaited their return. One by one, they came bounding through the lobby doors with excited faces and overflowing hearts. Each one, whether in a wealthy home, which was rare, or a very poor home, which was common, was touched by the love that had been shown to them and by the opportunity to share God's love with each family through Korean songs they had learned and gifts they had brought to share. Many said they'd never be the same, and some said they couldn't believe how the joy of obedience really worked when you allowed God to change your heart. When they returned home and gave testimonies at churches, they often told of this event and what God had taught them through it.

How often we miss the joy of obedience because we have preconceived ideas about what will or won't make us happy. First John 1:4 says "And these things we write, so that our joy may be made complete." It's obedience to God's Word that brings joy, and yet we find ourselves hanging on to houses, children, spouses, financial security, material things, thinking that they bring us fulfillment. Then when God opens a door for us to grow or to see His sufficiency, we complain or reject the idea altogether, and we'll never know what a difference we could have made in someone's life because of our obedience.

God was slowly, graciously revealing why He had moved us to the Pacific Northwest. He had people waiting. My husband was touching many lives—parents and students—at school and using his convictions and thirty-one years of Christian-school experience to excite and teach others about training students to the glory of God. My schedule was completely full of opportunities to share my faith and the joy of obedience and the pitfalls of disobedience. We were also enjoying the beauty of the Northwest, new friendships, and learning more of God's sufficiency in our lives. Our devotional times together were so rich and meaningful: sometimes because of the joys and sometimes because the challenges were so great that we were totally dependent upon God and His Word for reassurance, stability, and direction.

As weeks passed into months we received many letters, such as the following:

Dear Jim:

We have been praying for ten years that God would bring someone like you and Carol to this place. The first time we heard each of you speak we knew that God had brought you here for a specific reason. Thank you so much for leaving your family and comfortable situation to be used by God up here. The needs are great. Our children's lives have already been impacted by your example and leadership as well as our own. Thank you for coming.

Almost daily someone shared that we had been brought to Seattle just to meet a specific need or because they had prayed. You can't imagine how precious these words were, as they were a reminder that, so often, the joys of or whys of obedience come long after the initial step of obedience. For some, it's many years of faithful living and prayer, without seeing the fruit of it. But God's word is clear:

> Therefore, my beloved brethren, be steadfast, immovable, always abounding in the work of the Lord, knowing that your toil is not in vain in the Lord. (1 Cor. 15:58)

CHAPTER 8

A YEAR LATER

As we came to the end of our first year in Seattle, we were exhilarated with all God had accomplished, but we were also exhausted from the schedule and were greatly anticipating summer—a break from the pressures and a chance to visit our grandkids, kids, friends, and parents in California.

However, again things didn't go as we had planned. While on vacation in California, visiting our grandchildren, I had a medical problem which got progressively worse and resulted in my calling a doctor. He said I must immediately get home to my doctor and be examined, as my problem could be serious. We flew home that day, and I saw the doctor the following day. He discovered that I had two ovarian tumors that were of a size that greatly concerned him. He said they would schedule surgery right away. I left the doctor's office in shock and drove home to tell my husband the news. That dreaded word *cancer* had been mentioned and seemed to linger in my mind. Yet I didn't want to borrow tomorrow's problems today, so Jim and I again bound our hands and hearts together with prayer and committed the situation to the Lord. I desperately wanted to be victorious in the middle of this and not let the fear strike a blow.

I didn't know then that I would have to wait ten days for an available time in the operating room. I fought to keep my shield of faith in place during those ten days, as waiting is always difficult for me. But as I went into the operating room, I was at peace with whatever the outcome might be.

After several hours of surgery, my husband was informed that the tumors were benign, to the doctor's amazement. As I came out of my fog in the recovery room, the words "It wasn't cancerous!" were beautiful as my husband whispered them in my ear. I did have to have a complete hysterectomy, but that was fine and I was doing well.

What victory I felt as I was recovering! People came to visit, and I could share the peace God had given me before and during this trial. And I thought, *Wow, I'm doing pretty well in this area of trusting God through the difficult times.* I was so excited about the remaining summer because we had lost the previous summer to making the move to Seattle, and we'd had an incredibly busy year in our new ministry. We had greatly looked forward to spending time together, exploring the Northwest, relaxing together, and being refreshed for the new school year.

I left the hospital in three days and was proud of how well I was doing, both emotionally and physically. I began walking three or four blocks the next day and was eager to feel healthy and normal again, but day seven out of the hospital brought a new crisis for me to deal with. I suddenly couldn't keep anything in my body and had terrible cramping, and within eight hours from the onset, I was taken to the emergency ward because I had become so weak and faint. This was to begin an entire summer of illness and return visits to the emergency ward. It seems I had an infection in the intestines that no antibiotics would remedy. Each trip to the hospital meant more tests and new prescriptions to be taken for ten to fourteen days, only to end with another trip to the emergency ward at the end of the medication. While on the various drugs, I could only lay in bed and sip water or Gatorade. Absolutely everything else made me terribly sick, and my body rejected it immediately. It was during these months of lying in bed that I battled with the *giant of discouragement.*

Each morning as I awoke, I would be faced with thoughts, such as, *You're still sick—God didn't heal you overnight* or *You're never going to get well* or *You'll never be able to eat normally again* and so on. Each day was a battle for my mind as Satan bombarded me with discouragement and despair, and there was so little I could do to get my mind off of my illness and the hopelessness I felt. I knew I needed to change my thinking with God's help, or else Satan would have free run of my mind, and I'd fall into a giant pit that would be very destructive. So I began recalling the scriptures I'd learned from early childhood until now. I'd say them over and over and then ask God to show me how they could help me change my thinking from self-pity to single-minded trust.

As I prayed and began saying no to wrong thinking, the Lord opened up such encouraging words and thoughts for me, and I truly became excited about how His living word was beginning to heal my discouraged heart. First Peter 1:14–15 kept coming to my mind:

> As obedient children, do not be conformed to the former lusts which were yours in your ignorance, but like the Holy One who called you, *be holy yourselves also in all your behavior*. (emphasis added)

As the Holy Spirit moved in my heart, I realized that *I* was deciding when to have holy thoughts and when to have negative or angry thoughts. "All your behavior" meant even when sick, week after week. Therefore, I needed to figure out what it meant to have holy behavior while sick in bed.

Holy Behavior

Holy behavior meant not complaining! I could be obedient by doing four specific things that God laid on my heart:

1. *Not dwelling on the negative*

   > [T]hat you may walk in a manner worthy of the Lord, to please Him in all respects, bearing fruit in every good work and increasing in the knowledge of God: strengthened with all power, according to His glorious might, for the attaining of all steadfastness and patience. (Col. 1:10–11)

   I certainly couldn't please the Lord in all respects with my negative, discouraged, hopeless thoughts, and I wasn't calling on His *power* and *glorious might* to help me be steadfast. I knew that I needed to confess that I'd lost faith in His plan and was discouraged because I didn't like it or understand it. And again I asked God to help me truly desire to be holy in my behavior and thoughts, even if no one was around to see me and it was the beginning of the death of discouragement.

2. *Taking one day at a time.* My earliest thoughts each day had been about how long this would go on and would I live like this for months or even years since the doctors seemed so baffled by it?

   Be anxious for nothing, but in everything, by prayer and supplication, with thanksgiving let your requests be made known to God. And the peace of God which surpasses all comprehension, shall guard your hearts and your minds in Christ Jesus. (Phil. 4:6–7)

   Worry about tomorrow only exhausted and discouraged me for today and never brought about anything positive.

3. *Trusting God to see me through.* Admittedly, I was sometimes caught feeling forgotten and unloved by God. Of course, this was because my shield of faith was down, and I was relying on my emotions rather than the truth of God's word.

   And after you have suffered for a little while, the God of all grace, who called you to His eternal glory in Christ, will Himself perfect, confirm, strengthen and establish you. (1 Pet. 5:10)

I have loved you with an everlasting love. (Jer. 31:3)

4. *Using the experience to glorify God.* It was difficult to see how lying in bed, day after day, could glorify God. But as people would call to check up on me, I could see that my words could bring glory to God.

In this you greatly rejoice, even though now for a little while, if necessary, you have been distressed by various trials, that the proof of your faith, being more precious than gold which is perishable, even though tested by fire, may be found to result in praise and glory and honor at the revelation of Jesus Christ. (1 Pet. 1:6–7)

I could see that my faith was on trial and I really needed to be faithful during these very difficult days so that my reaction to this illness would be precious to my Lord.

A Sacrifice of Thanksgiving

Another verse that penetrated my thinking at this time was Psalm 116:17:

To Thee I shall offer a sacrifice of thanksgiving and call upon the name of the Lord.

The dictionary definition of *sacrifice* is "the forfeiture of something highly valued for something or someone valued more highly." Through this verse, I was called on to give up or sacrifice my desire for a healthy body (which I valued) for my desire to please the Lord (which I valued more highly). This really magnified the issue for me and revealed how important my health had become to me, and I began to offer a "sacrifice of thanksgiving"—that was, to be thankful for my situation and sacrifice my need to be well. I could still pray for healing, and I did each day, but I could no longer let it control my attitude.

Don't Be Entangled!

> No soldier in active service entangles himself in the affairs of everyday life that he may please the one who enlisted him. (2 Tim. 2:4)

There's so much in which we can become entangled and which displeases the Savior who enlisted us. Our schedules can easily entangle us so that there's just not time for prayer or Bible study or other things God might want us to be involved in. There's the desire for money and possessions that can drive us to work harder and longer and can keep us from right relationships and spending time with our spouse or children. Wanting that perfect, fit body that is on TV and in all the magazines can entangle us into putting exercise, workouts, or dieting before all else, and it consumes our mind and our focus. Admittedly, some of these things are good in moderation, but if they keep us from wholeheartedly serving the Lord and doing what He asks of us, then we are entangled by them.

I was caught up in wanting to be healthy and my desire to do all the things I longed to do during the summer months. I continually had to confess and refocus on pleasing the one who enlisted me. I could only do this if I made a conscientious choice to love my Lord above all else.

Many are the plans in a man's heart, but the counsel of the Lord, it will stand. (Prov. 19:21).

Continue to Bear Fruit

What an incredible encouragement Jeremiah 17:5–8 was to me as I recalled each phrase and meditated on it:

Cursed is the man who trusts in mankind and makes flesh his strength, and whose heart turns away from the Lord. For he will be like a bush in the desert and will not see when prosperity comes, but will live in stony wastes in the wilderness, a land of salt without inhabitant. Blessed is the man who trusts in the Lord and whose trust is the Lord. For he will be like a tree planted by the water, that extends its roots by a stream and will not fear when the heat comes; but its leaves will be green, and it will not be anxious in a year of drought, nor cease to yield fruit.

My first thought was that *cursed* or miserable is the one who tries to find happiness in self or others. The *flesh* referred to here shows the weakness or feebleness of skin without bones. People who live in the flesh have no strength at all, and when the storms of life come, there is nothing to help hold them up and they become like a "bush in the desert." This bush refers to a tamarisk—a dwarf juniper—which is a barren, useless, worthless shrub. Such individuals won't even recognize prosperity because their focus is on self and they are continually frustrated, wasting every opportunity for growth or fruit-bearing. As I laid there in my bed, without even enough energy to get up, I longed to really take hold of God's strength.

Secondly, there is a stark contrast with the second man mentioned here: "Blessed [or happy] is the one who trusts in the Lord and whose trust is the Lord." I could see right away, while lying on my back, the extreme necessity of trusting God for this moment, this hour, this day and not allowing self back in, not trying to figure things out or ask the question, why? My trust had to be, not only in the Lord, but also in who He was—my Redeemer, my Salvation, my Rock, my Shield, my Shepherd! I couldn't think that this illness was some cruel mistake.

THE OTHER SIDE

God is weaving day by day a pattern full of color,
Full of twists and turns galore that doesn't match another.

It may look like a big mistake when glancing at it here,
With knots and loose ends dangling, making patterns quite unclear.

Sometimes hopeless it may seem because it doesn't fit
With what you thought 'twas all about and what your life would knit.

But Sovereign God designs your days when in Him you abide.
And someday when you see His face, you'll see the other side.

—Carol Hopson

"For he will be like a tree planted by the water that extends its roots by a stream . . ." In other words, if I choose to plant my life and my thoughts in God's Word and in His promises for me, I will be strong in my faith and will have great stability in the midst of adversity, because my root system is deep and solid. And "when the heat comes"—sick-

ness, change of plans, disappointments, hurtful situations—
I can still be "green" or healthy, whole, and content. The
promise goes even further to say that even in "a year of
drought"—times when the circumstances seem impossible
and uncomfortable—our comfort and strength will come from
within because of our relationship with the Lord. The last
phrase encouraged me the most, as it promises that if I did
make the right choices, I would continue to bear fruit. That
fruit would be evident in my conversations with others, for I
would either praise God for His lovingkindness and faithfulness and trust Him to work all things out for my good, or I
would resent my illness and let others know how miserable I
was. Oh how I longed to be fruitful and faithful! That meant
saying, "Whatever you want Lord!"

Barbara Johnson wrote the following in her book *Splashes
of Joy in the Cesspools of Life*:

- W—Whoever You put in, or take out of my life . . .
- H—However You want things to end up, only You
  see the big picture.
- A—As much as I can take, Lord. You know me best
  because . . .
- T—Time is nothing to You. Help me to be patient.
- E—Everything is in Your hands . . . help me to let go!
- V—Victory comes with You as my Guide.
- E—Eternity with You will be worth it all!
- R—Restoration is mine through You.

Finally, after God had touched my life in a new, very
meaningful way, He again healed me through a doctor who
finally found the right treatment for my rampant infection.
Slowly, I began to heal and add one food to my diet each
three or four days. I prayed that I would never take another

meal for granted, and I knew that God had given me a new sensitivity to those who suffer physically for long periods of time. I had never understood the depth of their discouragement, but I knew that somehow He would use even this experience to help others.

Blessed be the God and Father of our Lord Jesus Christ, the Father of mercies and God of all comfort; Who comforts us in all our affliction so that we may be able to comfort those who are in any affliction with the comfort with which we ourselves are comforted by God. (2 Cor. 1:3–4)

CHAPTER 9

LIFE
GOES ON

We were into our second year in our new school and community, and now that I was able to get out again, the world looked bright. Everything began to seem familiar, and we knew lots more names and faces and had made some close friendships. We began to have favorite places to go in the Northwest and even enjoyed the changes in climate. The seasons were beautiful, and the many lakes, streams, and mountains were spectacular.

We went to almost all the school games, plays, choral programs, and events so that we could really be in touch with the students and parents and have a one-on-one contact with them. They were becoming our new family, since ours was in California, and we were thanking God for the bond we felt with them. We had students in our home and parent seminars and were very excited about what God was doing in our midst. We were so thankful to get glimpses of why God had chosen to move us.

As Christmas was approaching, we decided that we needed to invite our neighbors over for a Christmas dessert early in December, because our school schedule was so full that month. That meant we needed to get the tree early and get the house decorated and the baking done right away. Of course, I wanted a large, tall tree that would reach the ceiling in our living room, and so we went and cut down a beautiful nine-foot pine tree and brought it home. The trunk was still muddy as we unloaded it because we had cut it down in a rainstorm. My husband put it in the tree stand, brought it into the living room, filled it with two gallons of water, and made sure it was secure before I decorated it.

I had one day to decorate the tree and the house and bake goodies for the open house for thirty or forty people. Needless to say, every minute counted, and I was on quite a schedule to make sure it all got done. I wanted our home to look festive and warm, but I also wanted it to reflect our love for the Lord so that our neighbors would know that our home was different. We had also decided to give them each a Christmas card, enclosing a poem I had written about the true meaning of Christmas, along with a tract. This was tied with ribbon to a beautiful chocolate star so they would know it was something special and take note of it when they got home.

After several hours, the tree was done, and I was pleased with the outcome. Each year is a little different, and it's always a challenge to get that special look that I have in my mind. But this tree looked like the picture I'd imagined. I went about the other rooms, changing mantels, making centerpieces for tables, spreading fresh pine branches and holly berries, and unwrapping treasures to display from past Christmases. While doing this, I was thanking God for the opportunity to have my neighbors over, since almost all of them had responded that they'd like to come, and many of them didn't know each other, though they had lived in the neighborhood for many years. We were the newest ones in the neighborhood, but we definitely wanted to let our neighbors know that we were interested in them so we could build on this for future relationships.

After getting the house ready I was exhausted and decided to get up early and do the baking that I had planned to do on Saturday. I'd have to do it before church because the guests were coming about two o'clock in the afternoon and there wouldn't be time later. I had done some baking earlier, but I had several things I was going to make so they'd be fresh and really delicious. I wanted this day to be special. We had prayed about it many times and were excited about what God might do through us in our neighborhood.

Early Sunday morning, as I walked out to the living room and looked at my beautiful tree, I was so thankful to have completed all the decorating the day before, and I felt the tree looked truly special this year. While holding my cup of coffee and admiring my handiwork, the tree slowly went from upright to hitting the dining room table and then the floor with a thud, dumping the two-gallon base of dirty water on my off-white carpet. Silver balls shattered, precious ornaments broke and the lights went black! I stood paralyzed, not knowing whether to cry, scream, or start mopping. *Why did this have to happen when I was trying to do something the Lord wanted me to do—reach out to my neighbors? And I was so busy, and this was a sacrifice of my time.* Yes, those thoughts did rush through my mind while the tears flooded my eyes, and then I quickly remembered that Satan didn't want this gathering to happen and that he would do anything he could to discourage or defeat me.

With that reminder and a quick prayer for help from the Lord, my husband and I began the four-hour process of cleaning up all the broken pieces, cleaning and drying the carpet with hairdryers, redecorating the tree, restringing the lights, and yes, we still made it to a later service at church. However, the baking didn't get done, so my pride had to give in to Costco's array of goodies, and we were ready for the two-o'clock arrival.

The Lord showed me later that afternoon why this was so important. One family stayed behind when the others had left, and we were able to share the gospel with them at length. They had so many questions and were so open to what we had to share. Others responded very positively to the poem and tract, and I was so thankful that the fallen tree had not ruined the day. It had made me more aware of the battle and of my responsibility to be "steadfast, unmovable, always abounding in the work of the Lord, for our labor is not in vain, in the Lord."

I'm rather like Martha at times, wanting everything to be perfect. But God has used some humor and some difficult situations to teach me what's really important. It isn't how perfect the house or the tree looks or how special and home-made the food is. It's reaching out, caring, and showing God's love to people, even when things aren't the way you'd like them to be.

In the spring of our second year in Seattle, my sister-in-law, Susie, who had suffered with cancer for many years, took a turn for the worse, and we didn't know how much more time she would have. I loved Susie like a sister, since we had roomed together in college thirty-five years ago, had raised our children together, and had enjoyed a wonderful love and friendship over the years. I wanted to spend as much time as possible with her and my brother, Gerry, during those last difficult days. At the same time, Jim and I had promised to take another group of students to Korea for a mission trip. We were responsible for all the planning, care, supervision, and spiritual nurturing of these twenty-four kids. The trip had been planned for almost a year, and there was no one who could go in our place on short notice, so again I faced something that was not what I would have planned. I wanted to be home in case these were Susie's last days on earth with us, but I knew that I had to be faithful to the ministry God had called us to.

It was very difficult to trust that this would all work out for good. How could it be good if she died while I was in Korea, and I probably couldn't even get home for the funeral? How could I expect my brother and family to understand how much I wanted to be there with them at this time? Why did the trip have to be right now? I didn't have any answers, but I did have God's words:

BUT GOD, THIS WASN'T MY PLAN!

Set your mind on things above, not on things on the earth.
(Col. 3:2)

O Lord, Thou hast heard the desire of the humble; Thou
wilt strengthen their heart, Thou wilt incline Thine ear.
(Ps. 10:17)

In obedience to the Lord, we set out for our second trip
to Korea on April 4. The Lord did exceedingly above all we
could ask or think by allowing His love and His words to
flow out through us and through the students in hospitals,
churches, orphanages, schools, and universities. So many lives
were touched, and we were indeed grateful to God for allowing us to serve Him again in this way. Living with the students in a foreign country and sharing each moment of the
day brought many opportunities for growth, encouragement,
and greater commitment to our Lord. One student shared
with me on the way home that she had learned more on
these two trips about the Lord, His provision, and what it
truly meant to live for Him, moment by moment, than in
her whole educational experience. Again, I thanked the Lord
for where He had placed us and for the lives He brought into
our pathway.

During these two weeks, I couldn't receive word from
home, so I didn't know how Susie was doing. But I just kept
asking God to fill me with His peace. We arrived home on
Sunday, April 20, and on April 23, Susie was welcomed into
heaven. Her last audible words were "God is in control!" God
allowed Jim and me to be with her and her family the last

night before she died. It was a miracle of God's goodness to us. Seeing my brother trust the Lord completely and not waiver during this time of great suffering and heartache will be forever in my heart, and it was a tremendous testimony to everyone who knew and loved them.

CHAPTER 10

NOT AGAIN!

After attending memorial services in Canada and California for my precious sister-in-law, unpacking from our Korea trip, teaching Bible seminars at school, and recovering from jet lag, I was on my way to speak at a weekend women's retreat. They had asked me to speak on what to do "Somewhere Down the Road" when things don't go as we planned. I was very excited to speak on this topic, as I had lots of illustrations and verses God had used to teach me. I would use our move to Seattle and my summer of illness, as well as other times God had changed my plans. I went with great anticipation for what God would do in me and in the lives of the women who came, because He had taught me so much through this move and the surrounding circumstances.

Each session seemed to well up from my heart so that I could hardly wait to share what God had put there. The scriptures that I had memorized were ministering mightily to me as I shared them, and I felt the Holy Spirit working among the women. I was so thankful that God had taken me through many difficult times and had proven Himself faithful so that I had personal experiences to share. I desired to be transparent and vulnerable so God could use me, and I shared that I was praying that this summer would be a time of rest and refreshment, as the last two had been so difficult. One was spent leaving all I knew and loved behind and moving to Seattle, and the other I'd spent ill and entirely in bed, so I was really ready for a refreshing, normal summer with my husband.

Two days after I arrived home from that retreat, I got another phone call that would change our lives again. Due to very difficult circumstances brought upon my husband by those in authority over him, he felt it necessary to resign. I was in shock! I knew my husband did the only thing he could do before the Lord, but suddenly our world had collapsed. We had left everything to move here! We had accepted the call and had made a choice to love the work, the people, the ministry, and even the weather. And God was working mightily in students, parents, and teachers. Why, why, why would we be forced to leave the place God had so clearly called us to? Where were we to go, and what were we to do? It was too late to find work in school administration, as those positions are filled in the early spring, and this was the end of the school year.

Not Again!

As I sat alone in my living room, fear came over me like a dark cloud. My mind raced with questions. *What will our future hold? What if we lose our home? How will others understand what has happened? Was it a mistake to move here? Why was my husband treated this way? Why do we have to leave our new family? Why is Satan winning?* Then there were other thoughts, such as *I want to complain; I don't understand why; I'm too tired to handle this; This is too painful; I'm so disappointed in people,* and on it went. I had grown to love the place God had called us to and was just feeling like it was truly home. Jim and I had been so grateful to the Lord for the ministries He had provided for us. I had more speaking engagements than I could handle and was thrilled about speaking for the Lord each chance I had. My calendar was booked a year in advance because of God's faithfulness in giving me the desire of my heart—to share His Word. God had blessed in so many ways, and this just didn't make any sense at all.

This Isn't Easy, Lord!

This isn't very easy, Lord,
It's not what I had planned!
The situation I now face
Seems to have hit the fan!

The load is getting heavy
And my heart is filled with pain.
I need your loving comfort
To heal my soul again.

It seems so difficult to trust
When all around grows dark.

BUT GOD, THIS WASN'T MY PLAN!

But if I don't accept your will
I've truly missed the mark!

For you have said "Be not afraid!"
"The battle is not yours!"
And I must willingly obey
And through this trial endure.

I *will* decide to heed your voice
And trust you with my pain.
I *will* take up my shield of faith
And in your Word remain.

I cannot see why this must be
With human eyes of mine.
But I *will* leave it at your feet
And praise you ahead of time!

—Carol Hopson
May 26, 1998

But after my tears and my crying out to the Lord, He set my mind on the right path and put a desire within me to immediately start a journal of "Facing Fear with Faith." Each fear or thought that came to my mind needed to be faced with faith in the truth of God's Word. I felt so alone as I sat in my living room with my life all in disarray. I knew that obedience again would be my only salvation when my heart was breaking. I again would put God to the test.

Here are some of the thoughts that raced through my mind and the scriptures that God immediately gave me to comfort and sustain me. I will share them just as God gave them to me.

1. **Fear: My future is suddenly insecure!**

Faith:
For this reason I say to you, do not be anxious for your life, as to what you shall eat or what you shall drink, nor for your body as to what you shall put on. Is not life more than food and the body more than clothing? Look at the birds of the air . . . are you not worth more than they? But seek first His kingdom and His righteousness, and all these things shall be added to you. Therefore, do not be anxious or tomorrow; for tomorrow will care for itself. Each day has enough troubles of its own. (Matt. 6:25–26, 33–34)

Those who love Thy law have great peace and nothing causes them to stumble. (Ps. 119:165)

Was the future so important? To me it was, but now I was faced with having a heart attitude that pleased the Lord, one that trusted His words and His plan even though it made no sense to me—again! Could I leave the unknown, uncertain future in His hands and still be at peace? If I was truly a committed Christian I'd have to answer yes. I felt a little like the children of Israel. They had seen God work such mighty miracles on their behalf and yet when they'd come to another "Jordan" they'd wonder how they would ever make it across.

2. **Fear: I may lose my home!**

Faith:
Do not lay up for yourselves treasures upon earth, where moth and rust destroy, and where thieves break in and steal. But lay up for yourselves treasures in heaven, where

neither moth nor rust destroys and where thieves do not break in or steal . . . for where your treasure is, there will your heart be also. (Matt. 6:19–21)

Do not love the world nor the things in the world. If anyone loves the world the love of the Father is not in him. (1 John 2:15)

I was convicted with how much my home had come to mean to me. We had done some remodeling and lots of fixing up to make it "our home" and we were greatly enjoying it. We loved entertaining and it was a wonderful home for that, and it seemed perfect for housing the whole family when they came for a visit. Our family had all remarked on how much they loved coming to our home, because it really seemed like where we belonged and the grandchildren were always asking when they could come back to Nana and Papa's house. But I hadn't realized that I was getting more attached than I should, and God, in His gentle voice, was reminding me that my heart couldn't be set on the earthly treasure of my home.

3. **Fear: People won't understand, and I'm not free to explain.**

    Faith:
    If anyone suffers as a Christian, let him not feel ashamed, but in that name let him glorify God. . . . Therefore let all those who suffer according to the will of God entrust their souls to a faithful Creator in doing what is right. (1 Pet. 4:16, 19)

Humble yourselves therefore under the mighty hand of God, that He may exalt you at the proper time, casting all your anxiety upon Him, because He cares for you. (1 Pet. 5:6–7)

At times I wanted to shout from the mountaintops what had happened. I wanted to explain and fight back and reverse the situation, but what did God want me to do? He brought this verse to me the first day, entrust your soul "to a faithful Creator in doing what is right [just]." That's so much more difficult to actually do than it is to teach to others. I had been giving that for years to women whose husbands had left them or mistreated them and had shared it with others who had suffered because of some unjust situation. Now I was faced with a choice more difficult than I had ever expected.

4. **Fear: Was this a mistake or part of God's plan?**

Faith:
Trust in the Lord with all your heart and lean not on your own understanding. In all your ways acknowledge Him and He shall direct your paths. (Prov. 3:5–6)

Even from eternity I am He and there is none who can deliver out of my hand, I act and who can reverse it? (Isa. 43:13)

For I know the plans I have for you, declares the Lord, plans to prosper you and not to harm you, plans to give you hope and a future. (Jer. 29:11)

The Lord will accomplish what concerns me; Thy lovingkindness, O Lord, is everlasting; Do not forsake the works of Thy hands. (Ps. 138:8)

Remember that these are the verses as God gave them to me, one right after another. I did not search for them. He filled my thoughts with them so I could hardly write them down as fast as He gave them. So after I wrote them down, I would reflect on why He had given these specific verses for this specific fear or question. I was not to try to understand what had happened, only acknowledge that He was Lord of my life and that He would continue to accomplish what concerns me because of His lovingkindness toward me. This I had to accept by faith, not by emotion, because I certainly didn't feel, at this point, that this situation had come out of God's lovingkindness. But "without faith it is impossible to please God" (Heb. 11:6), so I knew I would have to trust implicitly and without reservation in His Word.

I also would have to believe that God had a "future and a hope" out there for us, even though it was in total darkness to me at this point. I thought it was too soon to stretch me like this again, as I had just really felt at home in the past few months. But trying to figure it out only caused frustration and doubt, so that definitely wasn't God's way for me.

5. **Fear: I feel like complaining!**

Faith:
Many are the afflictions of the righteous, but the Lord delivers him out of them all. . . . The Lord redeems the soul of His servants; and none of those who take refuge in Him will be condemned. (Ps. 34:19, 22)

I will bless the Lord at all times, His praise shall continually be in my mouth. (Ps. 34:1)

For in the day of trouble, He will conceal me in His tabernacle; in the secret place of His tent, He will hide me; He will lift me up on a rock. And now my head will be lifted up above my enemies around me, and I will offer in His tent, sacrifices with shouts of joy. I will sing, yes, I will sing praises to the Lord. (Ps. 27:5–6)

Would I ever feel like singing again? My Bible said I would! Could I truly "bless the Lord at all times" even when the pain was so deep? What a challenge for those times when we feel alone, betrayed, empty, and even angry. His praise certainly wasn't "continually in my mouth" on this day. But God knows that we are human, and He knew that I wanted to do the right thing, but it would take time to truly, wholeheartedly be joyful again.

6. **Fear: Satan is winning!**

Faith:
Be on the alert. Your adversary, the devil, prowls about like a roaring lion, seeking someone to devour. But resist him, firm in your faith, knowing that the same experiences of suffering are being accomplished by your brethren who are in the world. And after you have suffered for a little while, the God of all grace, who called you to His eternal glory in Christ, will Himself perfect, confirm, strengthen and establish you. (1 Pet. 5:8–10)

And the God of peace will soon crush Satan under your feet. (Rom. 16:20)

Now judgement is upon this world, now the ruler of this world shall be cast out. (John 12:31)

BUT GOD, THIS WASN'T MY PLAN!

I was so concerned about Satan's winning in the ministry we were involved in, that I almost lost sight of his winning a battle in my heart. The words *resist him* jumped out at me, and I knew that I couldn't leisurely dwell on the hurts of the situation or I would allow Satan a victory. That was something I definitely didn't want to happen.

DEAR GOD, IT HURTS!

Dear God, sometimes it hurts so much
To be your servant here.
Sometimes I feel I can't go on
Or shed another tear.

My ways are not your ways,
The Bible plainly states.
But oh, how difficult to trust
This isn't some mistake.

And then I think of how it hurt
For you to give your Son.
To see Him beaten, scorned, unloved,
So vict'ry could be won.

And then I feel so comforted
For You know how I feel.
You have not left me all alone,
Before You I shall kneel.

And leave my sorrows at your feet
To do with as you please.

> But help me think, when times are hard,
> To *first* go to my knees.
>
> —Carol Hopson

7. Fear: This is so unfair!

Faith:
For you have been called for this purpose, since Christ also suffered for you, leaving you an example for you to follow in His steps, who committed no sin, nor was any deceit found in His mouth. And while being reviled, He did not revile in return; and while suffering He uttered no threats, but kept entrusting Himself to Him who judges righteously. (1 Pet. 2:21–23)

Beloved, do not be surprised at the fiery ordeal among you, which comes upon you for your testing, as though some strange thing were happening to you. But to the degree that you share the sufferings of Christ, keep on rejoicing. (1 Pet. 4:12–13a)

Many are the plans in a man's heart, but the counsel of the Lord it will stand. (Prov. 19:21)

Why are we always so surprised when trials come our way? I think it's because we get so comfortable in our circumstances that we forget that this is not our home and that comfort is not the goal God has in mind for us. His plan for us is obedience and growth in any situation so that we might glorify Him. When we get too comfortable, even in doing very good things, we seem to forget that God has a different plan for His people. When I meditated on "for you have been called for this purpose, since Christ also suffered for you," I was struck with how off-track my thinking could get. Perfect or happy circumstances aren't what it's all about, but rather, accepting whatever circumstances God brings, with confident trust in His plan, is what brings glory to God. "That you might walk in a manner worthy of the Lord, to please *Him* in all respects" (Col. 1:10, emphasis added).

8. **Fear: This doesn't make any sense to me!**

Faith:
You turn things round. Shall the potter be considered as equal with the clay, that what is made shall say to its maker "He did not make me"? Or what is formed say to Him who formed him, "He has no understanding"? (Isa. 29:16)

But as for me, I trust in Thee, O Lord. I say, Thou art my God. My times are in your hands." (Ps. 31:14–15a)

My heart is steadfast, O God, my heart is steadfast; I will sing, yes I will sing praises!" (Ps. 57:7)

He who trusts in his own heart is a fool, but he who walks wisely will be delivered. (Prov. 28:26)

Trust in the Lord with all your heart and lean not on your own understanding. In all your ways acknowledge Him and He shall direct your paths. (Prov. 3:5–6)

Somehow, if it doesn't make sense to me, I feel it must not be right. That goes directly against what God says, and it is another reason why we can't rely on our emotions when we're faced with very difficult situations. Satan tried time and time again to trap me into this kind of thinking, which always led into a downward spiral. But reciting God's words over and over would dispel the doubt and my spirit would be revived.

9. **Fear: I'm too tired to handle this!**

Faith:
Do you not know, have you not heard? The everlasting God, the Lord, the Creator of the ends of the earth does not become weary or tired. His understanding is inscrutable. He gives strength to the weary, and to him who lacks might He increases power. Though youths grow weary and tired and vigorous young men stumble badly, yet those who wait for the Lord will gain new strength. They will mount up with wings like eagles. They will run and not get tired, they will walk and not become weary. (Isa. 40:28–31)

The sacrifices of God are a broken spirit; a broken and contrite heart, O God, Thou wilt not despise. (Ps. 51:17)

And let us not lose heart in doing good, for in due time we shall reap if we do not grow weary. (Gal. 6:9)

When we're tired it's easy to give in to bitterness, lack of faith, frustration, feeling overwhelmed and wanting to give up. But God's promises are just as true when we're tired as when we're invigorated, and we need to trust them more than ever at those times. It was a choice I had to make, moment by moment, to believe and trust that God would revive my heavy and weary heart.

10. Fear: This is too painful!

Faith:
For momentary, light affliction is producing for us an eternal weight of glory far beyond all comparison. (2 Cor. 4:17)

And He has said to me, My grace is sufficient for you, for power is perfected in weakness. Most gladly therefore, I will rather boast about my weaknesses, that the power of Christ may dwell in me. Therefore, I am well content with weaknesses, with insults, with distresses, with persecutions, with difficulties, for Christ's sake; for when I am weak, then I am strong. (2 Cor 12:9–10)

Faithful is He who calls you, and He also will bring it to pass. (1 Thess. 5:24)

Could I be content with weaknesses, with insults, with distresses and difficulties for Christ's sake? In my heart, I always wanted to be, but now the true depth of my love for my Lord would be revealed in the way I handled another change of plans. Would I fight against what God was allowing, or choose to offer my will as a love gift to Him and accept His plan?

ACCEPT IT?

Accept it?
    I don't like it!
        It's not the way I want it.

Accept it?
    I can't do it!
        I haven't got the strength.

Accept it?
    I don't want it!
        It's not what I had planned.

Accept it?
    You planned it?
        OK Lord! Take my hand!

—Carol Hopson

As I reflected on these fears and on the precious words of truth that God revealed to me as I went to Him in weakness and discouragement He did for me just as He did for David: "He revived me according to His Word" (Ps. 119:25, 107). It was only as I meditated on His Word and on His faithfulness in the past that I could face each new day with hope and confidence. Facing fear with faith was certainly the answer for me.

CHAPTER 11

THE YOKE OF REST

As the shock of our new circumstances wore off and as I allowed God to show me His purpose each day, He had incredible lessons to teach me. He was still using me to speak at many retreats and conferences, and I needed to be wholeheartedly His and at rest. When you're used to getting a salary, used to your husband having an office to go to, and used to knowing where you're headed, and then suddenly, all these things are gone, resting is not easy but becomes a daily choice. I found myself trying to figure out the next step. Should I go back to work full time? Could I somehow help Jim find a job in Seattle so we wouldn't have to move again? Could we start a business of our own and succeed? But I kept hearing that still, small voice say, *"Rest in the Lord and wait patiently for Him"* (Ps. 37:7).

I looked up all the verses I could find on rest, and the most familiar one kept speaking to me:

Come unto me all who are weary and heavy-laden, and I will give you rest. Take My yoke upon you, and learn from Me, for I am gentle and humble in heart and you shall find rest for your soul. (Matt. 11:28)

I had memorized this when I was a young child and thought it sounded really comforting, but what did it really mean for me today? How could putting on a yoke help me find rest? Since I like to dissect verses, phrase by phrase, I began studying each part as if I'd never read it before.

First of all, Jesus says, "Come unto *Me*" (emphasis added). I'm not to look for other solutions when I'm tired of the situation and weighted down with my problems. Jesus is the only One who can understand and lift the weight. I may try eating, shopping, running around to keep busy, spending time with friends, or worrying, but none of these things solves the problem or relieves my stress. He alone knows my heart and my needs, and He alone can give me rest.

"All you who are *weary* and *heavy-laden*" certainly depicted me at times (emphasis added). I was sometimes weary of my circumstances and weary of praying for the situation to change when I saw nothing changing. I was weary of obeying God and then having things not go as I expected them to go. At any moment I could be laden with worry, resentment, bitterness, or fear. So this passage certainly was for me.

"I will give you rest." He doesn't say *you will get* but *I will give*, showing His power and His personal involvement in my life when I come to Him, ready for His help. Rest isn't something I can acquire on my own, no matter how hard I try. True rest must come from My heavenly Father's hand as I put my hand in His.

The next portion is critical to our being able to rest, as it shows us we have a choice to make. *"Take* my yoke upon you" requires me to do something (emphasis added). Again, the Lord doesn't say, "I'll put my yoke upon you." He desires a response from me, and my taking of the yoke is an act of obedience, of giving up my will to His will. When I submit to His yoke of love, I am willing and ready to learn from Him as He has said—"and learn of Me." There's always so much I need to learn, but it begins with letting Him lead. When oxen are yoked together, there is always a leader and a follower. If I am trying to go my own way while yoked with my Lord, I will have pain, frustration, and very little progress. But when I submit to His leadership and course for my life, then I'll see progress, and when I cease going my own direction, life becomes so much easier, and rest is the result. This must begin in my thinking, first, and then work out into my words, actions, and reactions. *Being heavy-laden doesn't come from my circumstances but from fighting against God's plan and provision in my circumstances.*

My Lord is "gentle and humble in heart" and that is what I am to learn of Him as I am yoked with Him. I am to watch and read His example, how He reacted to the unfair treatment He received: "while suffering He uttered no threats but kept entrusting Himself to Him who judges righteously" (1 Pet. 2:23). He "emptied Himself" before going to the cross in humble and complete obedience to His Father (Phil. 2:5–8). His desire to please the Father superceded any other desire, and that must be the ultimate goal of my heart if I am to "find rest for my soul."

BUT GOD, THIS WASN'T MY PLAN!

"My yoke is easy and my load is light," Jesus said. I have Christ's example to follow and I need only to submit to his leading, not try to figure things out and make them work by myself. I also have the Holy Spirit's presence and comfort and the joy that comes from willing obedience. These things make the load so much lighter and I begin to have purpose again, to follow my Leader.

THE YOKE OF REST

"Take My Yoke upon you
And I will give you rest.
Give me all your burdens
And I'll give you My best. "

Why do we distrust this
And all our burdens bear?
Why do we still worry
And think God doesn't care?

Because we haven't trusted
His sovereignty above.
And we have not submitted to
His gentle yoke of love.

We look at all around us
And discontent sets in.
We do not claim His promises
And our hearts fill with sin.

Confession is the first step
To finding rest and peace.

THE YOKE OF REST

Then gladly take His yoke of love
And all your cares release.

Then God will do abundantly
More than words can say,
He'll give you His sufficient grace
For resting every day!

—Carol Hopson

CHAPTER 12

MY NEW SONG

As I come to this chapter, we are six months into not knowing what the future holds. So many friends have lovingly assured us that "I'm sure God has something so much better for you and it's just around the corner." But we can't be assured that it's just around the corner, because our timing isn't the same as God's timing. Nor can we be sure it's something so much better, because we don't know what God's next step for us is. If we are expecting what makes sense to us and what other people think should happen, we aren't truly open to *whatever* God desires for us.

BUT GOD, THIS WASN'T MY PLAN!

Remember when Ruth, in the Old Testament, returned to Bethlehem with Naomi after her husband died. She came to a foreign land, leaving all she knew behind, because God had led her to follow her mother-in-law and stay with her. As she returned, Naomi told her to go and glean in Boaz's field, and at the end of the barley season, she was instructed to go to the threshing floor and lie at Boaz's feet and wait. I'm sure that by this time, Ruth had great expectations of Boaz becoming her kinsman redeemer—the one who could provide everything she needed and make her feel worthy and secure again. He had been so kind to her and, as far as she knew, was her nearest kinsman. But as she waited for Boaz's reaction, he said,

> And now it is true I am a close relative; however, there is a relative closer than I. Remain this night, and when morning comes, if he will redeem you, good; let him redeem you. But if he does not wish to redeem you, then I will redeem you, as the Lord lives. Lie down until morning. (Ruth 3:12–13)

Ruth did as she was told, she set aside her expectations and disappointment and waited. In the morning, Boaz said to her,

> [G]ive me your cloak that is on you and hold it. So she held it and he measured six measures of barley and laid it on her. Then she went into the city. (Ruth 3:15)

This was not what Ruth expected; she wanted to be his wife, but she emptied herself of her plans and opened her cloak and gratefully received what Boaz gave her. She had to be willing to rest and receive—rest in God's timing and receive whatever His plan was. That is where I find myself right now. I am resting in God's arms and receiving the gifts He supplies on a daily basis. Some gifts are monetary, some are spoken words from friends, some are verses that revive my soul, some are special moments with my husband, some are unexpected joys, and always I have the special gift of His grace to meet each of my deepest needs.

While learning to rest and receive, I have truly been brought by God from the *pit to praise*, without my circumstances changing. Psalm 40:1–3 is such a clear testimony of my heart:

> I waited patiently for the Lord and He inclined to me and heard my cry. He brought me up out of the pit of destruction, out of the miry clay; and He set my feet upon a rock making my footsteps firm. And He put a new song in my mouth, a song of praise to our God. Many will see and fear and will trust in the Lord.

To wait patiently for the Lord means to wait for Him *alone* to bring relief and rest. I can't get my answers from others, from trying to change or fix the circumstances, and I can't have a certain outcome in mind and fix my hope on it. I need to wait patiently and completely on the Lord.

How grateful I am that "He inclined to me and heard my cry." I'm not just part of a mass of people that God is responsible for; I'm His precious lamb, and He, as my shepherd, inclines to me when I cry. He hears me just as the sheep hears his shepherd's voice and knows it above all the others. He is a personal God who cares deeply that I am in pain, and He is ready and eager to help me. He is never too busy with other problems, but is always immediately available to hear my cry for help.

As you've read through these chapters, you've seen that there have been many times that I've felt as if I had fallen into a pit and wondered how I would get out again. But this portion of God's precious Word always reminded me that He was the only one who could bring me out of the pit. "He brought me out of the pit of destruction . . ." There are many things that put us in an emotional pit; here are just a few:

1. Unconfessed sin—Psalm 32:3–5; Proverbs 28:13
2. Doubts about God's provision—Matthew 6:24–34
3. Bitterness—Hebrews 12:15; Psalm 139:23–24
4. Unresolved anger—Colossians 3:8; Psalm 51:10
5. Lack of contentment—2 Corinthians 12:9–10
6. Focusing on the circumstances—Psalm 16:8; 2 Chronicles 20:12

If you were in a physical pit in the ground and there was no way out, the more you tried to climb out, the more exhausted, tired, discouraged, and hopeless you would become. It's the same with our emotional pits; the more we try to work it out without God's help and without obedience to His Word, the more frustrated we become. *We always need a rescuer to bring us out of the pit.*

When we moved to Seattle, our granddaughter Becca was only two years old. She was used to seeing us often and staying at Nana and Papa's house and doing fun things together. When we left, she was too young to understand that we had moved to another state and wouldn't be able to see her nearly as often. Her only understanding was that Nana and Papa had disappeared! When we'd talk on the phone to her, she'd always ask, "Where *are* you, Nana?" with great emphasis on each word. It would break my heart that she couldn't understand why we couldn't be together.

Our first Christmas away, we decided to fly our children and grandchildren up to spend the holidays with us. Jim and I got to the airport one-and-a-half hours early to wait for their arrival, because we just couldn't stay home any longer. As their plane landed, I stationed myself at the top of the walkway that comes from the plane into the airport terminal. I wanted to see my grandchildren the earliest possible minute I could. Of course, they were the last ones off the plane. But all of a sudden, I saw these two little, blonde heads and saw our adorable grandson Elliot come around the corner and up the ramp. When they spotted me they began to run and seemed to even leave the ground. As Becca, Monica, and Elliot ran into my arms Becca was shaking with excitement and said, "Nana, Nana! I found you!"

Later on, as I lovingly recalled each moment of that day, I realized that I am sometimes like Becca. I have no understanding of what God is doing, and I seem to lose sight of Him because of it. He is not lost! He always knows where I am, just as I knew were my granddaughter was. Her excitement at finding me reminded me of the joy I feel when I am emotionally reunited with my heavenly Father. That is what I am feeling now as I am writing this chapter. I have truly found His loving arms outstretched to me saying, "I've always been here for you; you just lost sight of me for a little while."

After God brings us out of the pit, He puts our feet on a rock. As I have spent many hours at beaches in California, I've noticed the huge rocks just off the shore in many places. I've observed that no matter how many times those waves crash into the rocks they don't move or change. They stay the same day after day, year after year. That is what my Rock is like. My Lord never changes, He is consistent and reliable in all situations. I do not need to be thrown about emotionally by every circumstance if my feet are planted on the Rock of His love, His forgiveness, His promises, His plan for my future, His joy!

> I love Thee, O Lord, my strength. The Lord is my rock and my fortress and my deliverer, my God, my rock, in whom I take refuge; my shield and the horn of my salvation, my stronghold. (Ps. 18:1–2)

"And He put a new song in my mouth, a song of praise to our God." I love this part! God has always given me a new song after each trial or pit, and this experience is no different except that I'm singing louder and more often. As God has continued to bring many opportunities for me to speak at retreats, churches, and various seminars, my song is being heard by more people than I had ever dreamed possible. There are many who speak about their difficult circumstances after they have seen the other side of the mountain and are rejoicing in the wonderful new circumstances or position they have. *God has been showing me that I need to see God at work in my life right in the middle of the storm, when nothing has changed except my heart and my focus.* I kept wondering when I could finish this book with the final chapter of how God had provided work and how we were so excited about where God was taking us. But now I know that my "song" must be sung now, just like Jehoshaphat sang as the armies were coming to attack his people.

What is my new song? Oh, it's so wonderful, I hardly know how to put it into words. It's truly a song of praise to God because I no longer worry about tomorrow. I no longer think about the hurts and injustices of the situation. My heart is too full of God's love and grace in my life. He has given me so many opportunities to share with others who are hurting, share with them about how they can have His joy anytime when they choose to obey.

I no longer feel that I have to be near my grandchildren to be truly happy. I've learned that He will give me such joy when we're together that each moment is magnified and enjoyed so much that nothing is ever taken for granted anymore, like the week I was able to spend with my daughter, Jennifer, when our fourth grandchild Jack was born. What incredibly beautiful memories I have of every moment of that visit, which carry me through long weeks and months when we can't be together.

My song includes beautiful, wonderful memories of the things I left behind and gratitude for the new adventures I have faced. I have a new song because of new friends and their loving support and fellowship, new babes in Christ because God brought us to this place, restored families and relationships because God chose to use us as His servants. *My new song doesn't wait for things to change, but rather it thanks God ahead of time for His plan for me.* And there's a reoccurring theme that runs throughout my song, a new depth of understanding and appreciation of the sovereignty of God in my life. As long as my heart is fixed on pleasing and serving Him, and Him alone, I can trust Him to carry me through anything. The chorus of my new song resounds with gratitude because He has chosen to work in me and through me for His honor and glory!

Max Lucado tells the following story in His book entitled *In the Grip of Grace*:

> Here is the scene: You and I and a half dozen other folks are flying across the country in a chartered plane. All of a sudden the engine bursts into flames and the pilot rushes out of the cockpit.

"We're going to crash!" he yells. "We've got to bail out!"

Good thing he knows where the parachutes are because we don't. He passes them out, gives us a few pointers, and we stand in line as he throws open the door. The first passenger steps up to the door and shouts over the wind, "Could I make a request?"

"Sure, what is it?"

"Any way I could get a pink parachute?"

The pilot shakes his head in disbelief. "Isn't it enough that I gave you a parachute at all?" And so the first passenger jumps.

The second steps to the door. "I'm wondering if there is any way you could ensure me that I won't get nauseated during the fall?"

"No, but I can ensure that you will have a parachute for the fall."

Each of us comes with a request and receives a parachute.

"Please captain," says one, "I am afraid of heights. Would you remove my fear?"

"No," he replies, "but I'll give you a parachute."

Another pleads for a different strategy, "Couldn't you change the plans? Let's crash with the plane. We might survive."

The pilot smiles and says, "You don't know what you are asking," and gently shoves the fellow out the door. One passenger wants some goggles, another wants boots, another wants to wait until the plane is closer to the ground.

"You people don't understand," the pilot shouts as he "helps" us, one by one. "I've given you a parachute; that is enough."

Only one item is necessary for the jump, and he provides it. He places the strategic tool in our hands. The gift is adequate. But are we content? No. We are restless, anxious, even demanding.

Too crazy to be possible? Maybe in a plane with pilots and parachutes, but on earth with people and grace? God hears thousands of appeals per second. Some are legitimate. We, too, ask God to remove the fear or change the plans. He usually answers with a gentle shove that leaves us airborne and suspended by His grace.

This is where I find myself . . . contentedly suspended by His grace with a new song in my heart.

My New Song

At first I couldn't sing a note,
no song was in my heart.
I felt betrayed, deserted,
my life had come apart!

Satan saw my circumstance
and recognized my pain,
And thought "Aha, a victory,
another 'saint' I'll claim!"

But knowing that the choice was mine,
to get my shield in place
I ran to God and started in
on "facing fear with faith."

The pages of my journal
saw God's truths come alive
And I knew that my only hope
was in Him to abide.

BUT GOD, THIS WASN'T MY PLAN!

As I began this walk of faith,
again *not what I planned*,
I saw how lovingly He came
and took hold of my hand.

He guided me through unknown doors,
and held me when I cried.
He helped me leave the hurt with Him
and said "I'm on your side."

I don't know when my new song came
or how it got its start.
I only know that gradually,
it flowed out from my heart.

I'll bless the Lord through all my times,
my days are in His hands
And I will serve Him faithfully,
though *not as I had planned*.

For He is sovereign, He is God,
the Potter . . . I'm the clay.
And I have found that true joy comes
when I choose to obey.

So I sing because He's faithful,
and I sing because I'm free,
for what My Father has in store
is what is best for me!

—Carol Hopson

EPILOGUE

It's been almost six months since I submitted my manuscript to the publisher and I am now in the final editing process. As I finish up all the details necessary for publication, I'm reminded of God's faithfulness and provision during these months of living by faith and not by sight. It has been my constant prayer that God would use me to continue to bear fruit and not be anxious in this "year of drought".

> "Blessed is the man who trusts in the Lord and whose trust is the Lord, for he will be like a tree planted by the water, that extends its roots by a stream and will not fear when the heat comes; but its leaves will be green. And it will not be anxious in a year of drought nor cease to yield fruit." (Jeremiah 17:7,8)

As you know, I chose to end this book not knowing where God was leading us but resting in His plan for us. Three weeks ago, after waiting almost 12 months for direction, God "directed our path" and gave us "the desire of our hearts" in an amazing way.

In a period of 48 hours God did the following:

- He gave us the ministry we had truly desired out of all the possibilities we had been open to...
- He sold our house to the first people that walked in...
- He found a house for us that is exactly what we needed...
- He moved us within two hours of our children & grandchildren..
- He provided an incredible built-in sport-court and play set in our yard for all ages of our grandchildren to enjoy...

and

- He gave us willing and eager hearts to serve Him in this wonderful new school near San Diego, California.

To God be the glory, great things He hath done!

To order additional copies of

BUT *God...*

This
Wasn't
My
Plan!

Please contact Carol Hopson at:

1015 Olive Crest Dr.
Encinitas, CA 92024
(760) 942-6812

Other books by Carol Hopson include:

But God, I'm Tired of Waiting!
Peace in the Midst
My Day, His Way